EXODUS

ENTER GOD'S STORY

EXODUS

ENTER GOD'S STORY

STORYTELLER

Lifeway Press®
Nashville, Tennessee

Editorial Team

Fiona Soltis
Devotional writer

Angel Prohaska
Associate Editor

Reid Patton
Senior Editor

Jon Rodda
Art Director

Tyler Quillet
Managing Editor

Joel Polk
Publisher, Small Group Publishing

Brian Daniel
Director, Adult Ministry Publishing

ISBN: 978-1-0877-6334-7 • Item number: 005837543
Dewey decimal classification: 222.12 • Subject heading: BIBLE. O.T. EXODUS 1-15 / EXODUS, THE / SALVATION

To order additional copies of this resource, write to Lifeway Resources Customer Service; 200 Powell Place, Suite 100, Brentwood, TN 37027; fax 615-251-5933; call toll free 800-458-2772; order online at Lifeway.com; or email orderentry@lifeway.com.

Printed in the United States of America

Adult Ministry Publishing • Lifeway Resources • 200 Powell Place • Brentwood, TN 37027

CONTENTS

ABOUT STORYTELLER

God could've chosen to reveal Himself in any way that He desired, yet in His wisdom, He chose to reveal Himself in the context of a story. We come to know and understand this reality as we immerse ourselves in the Scriptures and begin to see the entirety of Scripture as one interconnected story. By becoming familiar with the individual stories of Scripture, we train ourselves to see each as one part of God's big story.

Storyteller is a six week devotional and group Bible study experience designed to take people through Scripture in a way that is beautiful, intuitive, and interactive. Each volume uses a book of the Bible or a portion of Scripture from within a book to examine a key theme. This theme guides the Bible study experience and gives readers handles to help understand and digest what they're reading.

At the end of each study, you should have a deeper understanding of God, His Word, the big themes of Scripture, the connectedness of God's story, and His work in your life.

Let's enter the story together.

ABOUT EXODUS

TITLE

The title *Exodus* comes from a Greek word that means "departure" which is a reference to the central event of the book—the Israelites' exodus from Egyptian enslavement. The Hebrew title for Exodus is *Names* because it is the first word of the book in the original language.

THEME

The theme of Exodus is redemption. The events of the book lead up to and come away from God redeeming Israel from slavery and establishing a chosen nation to serve and represent Him in the world.

AUTHOR AND DATE

The book of Exodus, like the other books in the Pentateuch (Genesis, Exodus, Leviticus, Numbers, and Deuteronomy), was written by Moses. The book was written sometime after the exodus in 1446 BC and before the death of Moses in 1406 BC.

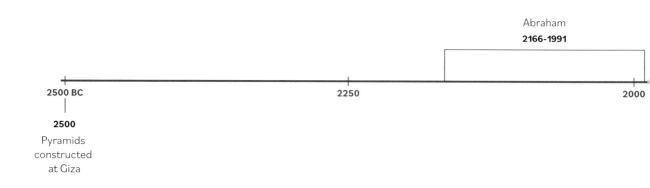

Abraham
2166-1991

2500 BC   2250   2000

2500
Pyramids
constructed
at Giza

SIMPLIFIED OUTLINE OF EXODUS

1:1–19:2   The Israelites are delivered from slavery.

19:3–24:8 God establishes a covenant with Israel and gives the Ten Commandments.

25–31   God provides instructions to build the tabernacle so that He may dwell
           with His people.

32–34   Israel breaks their covenant with God, yet He renews it.

35–40   The people of Israel construct the tabernacle.[1]

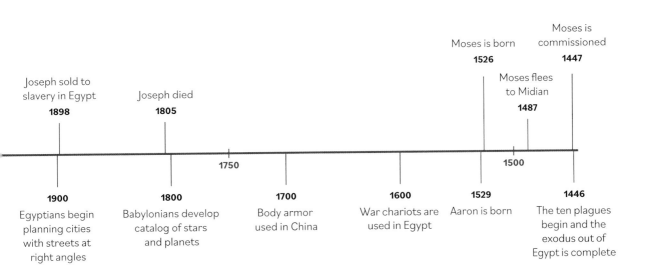

Joseph sold to slavery in Egypt
1898

Joseph died
1805

Moses is born
1526

Moses is commissioned
1447

Moses flees to Midian
1487

1750

1500

1900
Egyptians begin planning cities with streets at right angles

1800
Babylonians develop catalog of stars and planets

1700
Body armor used in China

1600
War chariots are used in Egypt

1529
Aaron is born

1446
The ten plagues begin and the exodus out of Egypt is complete

POSSIBLE ROUTES OF THE EXODUS

We know that when the Israelites left Egypt they headed towards Mount Sinai to meet with God and worship Him. Because there is some doubt as to where the biblical Mount Sinai is located, archeologists and biblical scholars have proposed several possible routes the Israelites could've taken out of Egypt. These routes are illustrated on the next page.[2]

THE DATE OF THE EXODUS

Based on biblical evidence we can conclude that the exodus from Egypt occurred in 1446 BC. According to 1 Kings 6:1, the exodus occurred 480 years before Solomon's fourth year as king, which in conjunction with other biblical information can be dated to 966 BC. Additionally, in Judges 11:26 Jephthah said that Israel had been living in regions of Palestine for 300 years. Jephthah lived around 1100 BC, thus dating the end of the wilderness journey to around 1400 BC.

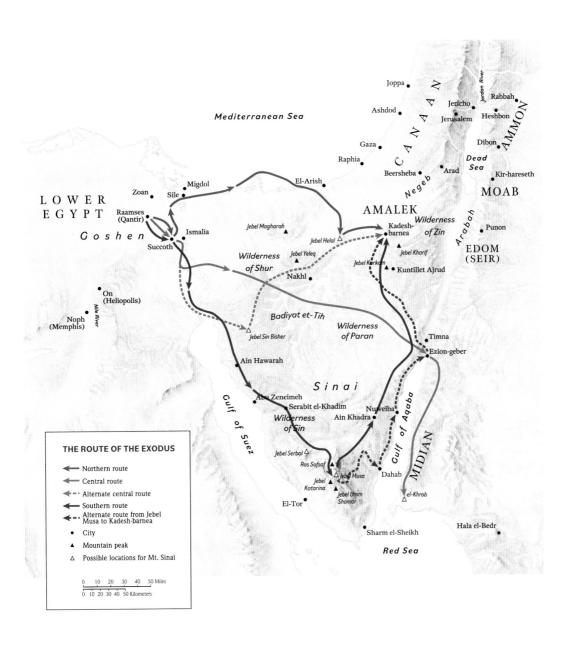

THE ROUTE OF THE EXODUS

⬅ Northern route
⬅ Central route
⬅- - Alternate central route
⬅ Southern route
⬅- - Alternate route from Jebel
　　 Musa to Kadesh-barnea
● City
▲ Mountain peak
△ Possible locations for Mt. Sinai

0　10　20　30　40　50 Miles
0　10　20　30　40　50 Kilometers

WHY STUDY EXODUS?

Exodus is the Rosetta stone for unlocking the Old Testament and the thread of redemption throughout Scripture. If you're looking for the thread of redemption throughout the Bible, there's no better place to start than in Exodus.

Consider what Christopher Wright has to say in *The Mission of God*.

> If you had asked a devout Israelite in the Old Testament period, "Are you redeemed?" the answer would have been a most definite yes. And if you had asked "How do you know?" you would be taken aside to sit down somewhere while your friend recounted a long and exciting story—the story of exodus. For indeed it is the exodus that provided the primary model of God's idea of redemption, not just in the Old Testament but even in the New, where it is used as one of the keys to understanding the meaning of the cross of Christ.[3]

Over six weeks, we will walk together through the first fifteen chapters of Exodus as God heard the cries of His people, responded by sending a deliverer, and gave us a pattern for recognizing His work in the world.

1. The information on this page is adapted from *The CSB Study Bible*, Dorian G. Coover-Cox, "Exodus," in *CSB Study Bible*: Notes, ed. Edwin A. Blum and Trevin Wax (Nashville, TN: Holman Bible Publishers, 2017), 87–89.
2. Thomas V. Brisco, *Holman Bible Atlas*, Holman Reference (Nashville, TN: Broadman & Holman Publishers, 1998), 68.
3. Christopher J. H. Wright, *The Mission of God.* (Downers Grove: IVP Academic, 2006), 256.

HOW TO USE THIS STUDY

Each week follows a repeated rhythm to guide you in your study of Exodus and was crafted with lots of white space and photographic imagery to facilitate a time of reflection on Scripture.

The week begins with an introduction to the themes of the week. Throughout each week you'll find Scripture readings, devotions, and beautiful imagery to guide your time.

Each week includes five days of Scripture reading along with a short devotional thought and three questions to process what you've read.

The Scripture reading is printed out for you with plenty of space for you to take notes, circle, underline, and interact with the passage.

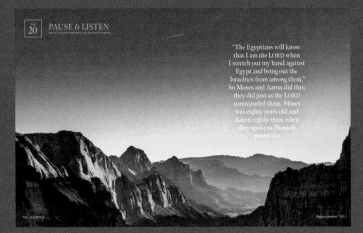

The sixth day contains no reading beyond a couple of verses to give you time to pause and listen to what God has said through the Scriptures this week. You may be tempted to skip this day all together, but resist this temptation. Sit and be quiet with God—even if it's only for a few minutes.

The seventh day each week offers a list of open-ended questions that apply to any passage of Scripture. Use this day to reflect on your own or meet with a group to discuss what you've learned. Take intentional time to remember and reflect on what the story of Exodus is teaching you.

The Plagues of Egypt

Throughout each week of study, you will notice callout boxes or supplemental pages provided to give greater context and clarity to the Scripture you're reading. These features will help you connect Exodus to the bigger story of Scripture.

LEADING A GROUP

Each week of study contains a set of questions that can be used for small group meetings. These open-ended questions are meant to guide discussion of the week's Scripture passage. No matter the size of your group, here are some helpful tips for guiding discussion.

PREPARE

REVIEW the Scripture and your answers to the week's questions ahead of time.

PRAY over your group as well as the Scriptures you've been studying. Ask God's Spirit for help to lead the group deeper into God's truth and deeper in relationship with one another.

MINIMIZE DISTRACTIONS

We live in a time when our attention is increasingly divided. Try to see your group time as a space and respite from the digital clutter—from scrolling, notifications, likes, and newsfeeds. Commit to one another to give focused time and attention to the discussion at hand and minimize outside distractions. Help people focus on what's most important: connecting with God, with the Bible, and with one another.

ENCOURAGE DISCUSSION

A good small group experience has the following characteristics.

EVERYONE IS INCLUDED. Your goal is to foster a community where people are welcome just as they are but encouraged to grow spiritually.

EVERYONE PARTICIPATES. Encourage everyone to ask questions, share, or read aloud.

NO ONE DOMINATES. Even though you may be "leading" the group, try to see yourself as a participant steering the conversation rather than a teacher imparting information.

DON'T RUSH. Don't feel that a moment of silence is a bad thing. People may need time, and we should be glad to give it to them. Don't feel like you have to ask all the questions or stay away from questions that aren't included. Be sensitive to the Holy Spirit and to one another. Take your time.

INPUT IS AFFIRMED AND FOLLOWED UP. Make sure you point out something true or helpful in a response. Don't just move on. Build community with follow-up questions, asking other people to share when they have experienced similar things or how a truth has shaped their understanding of God and the Scripture you're studying. Conversation stalls when people feel that you don't want to hear their answers or that you're looking for only a certain answer. Engagement and affirmation keeps the conversation going.

GOD AND HIS WORD ARE CENTRAL. The questions in this study are meant to steer the conversation back to God, His Word, and the work of the gospel in our lives. Opinions and experiences are valuable and can be helpful, but God is the center of the Bible, the center of our story, and should be the center of our discussion. Trust Him to lead the discussion. Continually point people to the Word and to active steps of faith.

KEEP CONNECTING

Spiritual growth occurs in the context of community. Think of ways to connect with group members during the week. Your group will be more enjoyable the more you get to know one another through time spent outside of an official group meeting. The more people are comfortable with and involved in one another's lives, the more they'll look forward to being together. When people move beyond being friendly to truly being friends who form a community, they come to each session eager to engage instead of merely attending. Reserve time each week to touch base with individual group members.

WEEK 1

A PROBLEM &
A PROMISE

Enter the story.

Entering the story of Exodus, you quickly realize the people of Israel have a problem. They are enslaved by a king who did not know about the Israelite man, Joseph, who once oversaw the entire Egyptian empire. But as you continue through Exodus, you will find it is also a book about a promise.

A promise of freedom and redemption.

And yet.

Every day God's people languished, God had a plan for delivering His people. He was in the details, preparing the way for their redemption. He worked through men and mighty miracles to free the Israelites from the Egyptians who enslaved them. He worked to free them from themselves.

The story of Exodus is rich with present-day promise and relevance—especially for anyone, anywhere, who has ever felt stuck. Anyone who has stood in faith or fallen in brokenness. Anyone longing to see a promise kept or begin a new day.

And who hasn't?

Just like He was for the Israelites, God—the same yesterday, today and forever—is present in our problems waiting to fulfill His promises. Now, as then, He is working in the details of our lives, preparing the way for ultimate redemption.

Ready for a closer look?

EXODUS 1:8-14

[8] A new king, who did not know about Joseph, came to power in Egypt. [9] He said to his people, "Look, the Israelite people are more numerous and powerful than we are. [10] Come, let's deal shrewdly with them; otherwise they will multiply further, and when war breaks out, they will join our enemies, fight against us, and leave the country." [11] So the Egyptians assigned taskmasters over the Israelites to oppress them with forced labor. They built Pithom and Rameses as supply cities for Pharaoh. [12] But the more they oppressed them, the more they multiplied and spread so that the Egyptians came to dread the Israelites. [13] They worked the Israelites ruthlessly [14] and made their lives bitter with difficult labor in brick and mortar and in all kinds of fieldwork. They ruthlessly imposed all this work on them.

RUTHLESS DEMANDS

The new king of Egypt was feeling threatened. The Israelites were overtaking his nation. Joseph, the great Jewish leader under a previous Pharaoh, had invited them to come. But much time had passed; generations had continued. The new king didn't know their history or understand their lineage. Frankly, he didn't care.

All he knew was that there were too many Israelites, and they were too strong. These Israelites worshiped only one God, while the Egyptians worshiped many. Could they overrun his kingdom? Could they steal away his power? Fear can make a man mean. It can rule the emotions and justify the unjustifiable.

The king enslaved the Israelites and appointed brutal slave drivers to wear them down with crushing labor. That way, he could show them who's "boss." But the more the king oppressed them, the more the Israelites multiplied and spread. The more they multiplied, the more oppressive the king became. The Bible tells us the Egyptians treated the Israelites without mercy, made their lives bitter, and were ruthless with demands.

Imagine it: unbearable oppression, seemingly no way out. And things were about to get worse. We don't yet know how the Israelites felt about their suffering. All the story has told us so far is about a hard-hearted king who ruled out of fear and anger. Yet lurking in the details of these verses of oppression is the promise God made long ago to make His people into a great nation as numerous as the stars in the sky or the grains of sand on a shore.

You may read this and feel like God had forgotten Israel. You may come to these verses feeling like God has forgotten you. Yet despite what is happening in the foreground, God is at work in the background.

God had a plan for delivering His people.

REFLECTIONS

What made Pharaoh feel threatened? How did he respond? Why does feeling threatened lead us to make poor choices?

These verses show God at work in the background of the story. What are some ways God operates in the background of our lives?

How might learning to find those instances where God is working in the background help you to trust God when it seems or feels like He is absent?

TRACING THE STORY

Reading Exodus is joining a story already in progress. It is the second book of the Bible and picks up where Genesis, the first book of the Bible, left off.

The majority of Genesis traces the family history of a man named Abraham. Joseph referred to in Exodus 1:8 is Abraham's great-grandson. His story is found in Genesis chapters 37–50.

EXODUS 1:15-22

¹⁵ The king of Egypt said to the Hebrew midwives — the first, whose name was Shiphrah, and the second, whose name was Puah — ¹⁶ "When you help the Hebrew women give birth, observe them as they deliver. If the child is a son, kill him, but if it's a daughter, she may live." ¹⁷ The midwives, however, feared God and did not do as the king of Egypt had told them; they let the boys live. ¹⁸ So the king of Egypt summoned the midwives and asked them, "Why have you done this and let the boys live?"

¹⁹ The midwives said to Pharaoh, "The Hebrew women are not like the Egyptian women, for they are vigorous and give birth before the midwife can get to them."

²⁰ So God was good to the midwives, and the people multiplied and became very numerous. ²¹ Since the midwives feared God, he gave them families. ²² Pharaoh then commanded all his people, "You must throw every son born to the Hebrews into the Nile, but let every daughter live."

DEFYING AUTHORITY

The king's anger continued to burn. It was no longer enough to just punish the Israelites. His anger and paranoia took him further.

He pulled aside a couple of Hebrew midwives and ordered them to kill any boy born to the Hebrews. Killing the Hebrew boys would prevent them from becoming men who could outnumber and overpower the Egyptians. But Shiphrah and Puah worshiped God and chose to obey Him rather than the King of Egypt.

When the king discovered that the boys were still alive, the midwives defended themselves by telling the king that Hebrew women were so vigorous that they delivered before the midwives could even get there. Was this true? The Bible does not tell us. We do know that God honored these women and their intent to protect the Hebrew babies.

God used the faithfulness of these two women to move His story of deliverance forward. If the midwives had gone along with the king's plan, the king wouldn't have had to escalate the situation further. However, once his plot with the midwives failed, Pharaoh took his rage a step further—he commanded his people to throw every Hebrew baby boy into the Nile. He was unthreatened by the daughters, even though he had just been outwitted by two women.

At Pharaoh's command, the Nile—the river that brought vitality and fertility to all of Egypt—would become a graveyard for Hebrew boys. And yet, even in this dark turn of events, God was at work. The king's order would lead to a crucial turn of events for one baby boy in particular: Moses. The edict ended up placing this baby exactly where he needed to be, at exactly the right moment, to fulfill the role God planned for him before time began.

And yet, even in this dark turn of events,
God was at work.

REFLECTIONS

INSIGHTS

The book of Exodus was originally written in Hebrew. In Hebrew, the book is called *Names* because it's the first word in the book. In our English translation it reads, "These are the names."

Names figure prominently in the story of Exodus. In this book, we first learn the personal name of God—Yahweh—when God discloses it to Moses. So it is not by accident that we never learn Pharoah's proper name, yet we know the name of two Hebrew midwives—Shiphrah and Puah.

What does this insight about the Hebrew midwives teach us about what God values?

When has God led you to take a stand for what is right even thought it was unpopular?

In what ways did God show up to support and empower you or impact the outcome?

EXODUS 2:1-10

MOSES'S BIRTH AND ADOPTION

2 Now a man from the family of Levi married a Levite woman. ² The woman became pregnant and gave birth to a son; when she saw that he was beautiful, she hid him for three months. ³ But when she could no longer hide him, she got a papyrus basket for him and coated it with asphalt and pitch. She placed the child in it and set it among the reeds by the bank of the Nile. ⁴ Then his sister stood at a distance in order to see what would happen to him.

⁵ Pharaoh's daughter went down to bathe at the Nile while her servant girls walked along the riverbank. She saw the basket among the reeds, sent her slave girl, took it, ⁶ opened it, and saw him, the child — and there he was, a little boy, crying. She felt sorry for him and said, "This is one of the Hebrew boys."

⁷ Then his sister said to Pharaoh's daughter, "Should I go and call a Hebrew woman who is nursing to nurse the boy for you?"

⁸ "Go," Pharaoh's daughter told her. So the girl went and called the boy's mother. ⁹ Then Pharaoh's daughter said to her, "Take this child and nurse him for me, and I will pay your wages." So the woman took the boy and nursed him. ¹⁰ When the child grew older, she brought him to Pharaoh's daughter, and he became her son. She named him Moses, "Because," she said, "I drew him out of the water."

DIVINE COINCIDENCE

God continued to play the long game in this journey to deliverance. There were simply too many "coincidences" along the way to believe otherwise.

At the same time Egypt's homicidal king decreed that all Hebrew boys should be throw into the Nile, God brought together an ordinary couple who had a special son—the Bible tells us he was "beautiful." His mother hid him for as long as she could, then made a special basket to help him float on the Nile waters.

Was it a coincidence that this woman might know how to make such a basket to hide him among the reeds? Was it chance that she might also have a daughter, old enough to stand nearby and watch what was happening? And was it just happenstance that the first person to see the baby in the basket might be an Egyptian princess who would feel compassion for him and raise him as her own?

God carefully orchestrated the events of Moses's life to lead to this moment. He was delivered from the Nile, found by an Egyptian princess, and nursed through infancy by his own Hebrew mother in an almost-too-fantastic-to-be-true moment.

The experiences this Moses would have in the palace would prepare him for the years to come in a way that nobody could have imagined. The story of Exodus is a story of God who is at work in every detail to bring about His intended result.

The story of Exodus is a story of
God who is at work in every detail to
bring about His intended result.

REFLECTIONS

What steps did God take to ensure that Moses survived Pharaoh's attempts to kill the Hebrew boys?

What seemingly "coincidental" events in your life has God used to bring you to the place
He wants you to be?

What are some ways we might keep our eyes open to see God's faithfulness in the overlooked
details of our lives? Give specific examples from the last year.

EXODUS 2:11-22

MOSES IN MIDIAN

[11] Years later, after Moses had grown up, he went out to his own people and observed their forced labor. He saw an Egyptian striking a Hebrew, one of his people. [12] Looking all around and seeing no one, he struck the Egyptian dead and hid him in the sand. [13] The next day he went out and saw two Hebrews fighting. He asked the one in the wrong, "Why are you attacking your neighbor?"

[14] "Who made you a commander and judge over us?" the man replied. "Are you planning to kill me as you killed the Egyptian?"

Then Moses became afraid and thought, "What I did is certainly known."

[15] When Pharaoh heard about this, he tried to kill Moses. But Moses fled from Pharaoh and went to live in the land of Midian, and sat down by a well.

[16] Now the priest of Midian had seven daughters. They came to draw water and filled the troughs to water their father's flock. [17] Then some shepherds arrived and drove them away, but Moses came to their rescue and watered their flock. [18] When they returned to their father Reuel, he asked, "Why have you come back so quickly today?"

[19] They answered, "An Egyptian rescued us from the shepherds. He even drew water for us and watered the flock."

[20] "So where is he?" he asked his daughters. "Why then did you leave the man behind? Invite him to eat dinner."

[21] Moses agreed to stay with the man, and he gave his daughter Zipporah to Moses in marriage. [22] She gave birth to a son whom he named Gershom, for he said, "I have been a resident alien in a foreign land."

THE DESERT

The book of Exodus covers many years. Some we experience in detail, but others pass by without a mention. Moses's time in the palace of the king is one such season.

Surrounded by power and opportunity, Moses would have been trained in all the wisdom of Egypt—the most educated, sophisticated culture of that time. He would've inherited an understanding of the Egyptians that would serve him well in his future dealings with Egypt.

At this point, he was forty years old.

And it would take another forty years in a completely different atmosphere to complete his training—and to place him at another precise moment in history. We find him going out to visit his own people—and seeing how harshly the Egyptians were treating them.

In a moment of anger, this still immature leader lashed out. Seeing an Egyptian beating a fellow Hebrew, Moses looked to make sure nobody was watching, killed the Egyptian, and hid the body in the sand. Moses tried to become a deliverer before God made him into a deliverer. The next day, he learned that his secret was out. He was seen. Worse yet, the king heard of his actions, and tried to kill Moses.

Moses escaped to Midian, where he began life as a shepherd. It is here that he met Zipporah, who would become his wife, and Zipporah's father, Jethro, who would prove to be a wise advisor. Even as he fled to escape punishment, God still saw, and still moved on his behalf.

Moses continued to trust God. But he also knew he was not yet where he was supposed to be; he was, by his own admission, a foreigner in a foreign land, waiting for God to move.

Moses was waiting for God to move.

REFLECTIONS

In these verses Moses is involved in two physical altercations. What is the difference between these two events?

Moses had entered a period of waiting. Why can waiting be so hard on our souls?

How might God use delayed deliverance, like waiting or some time in a "desert," to actually build your faith?

Connecting the Story

Exodus is one of the central stories of the Bible. Many themes found in Exodus echo in other parts of Scripture. Here are a few from this week's reading. Consider looking them up and reading them for yourselves.

EXODUS 1:7
The Israelites
increased in Egypt

GENESIS 15:5
God promised Abraham his
descendants (the Israelites) would
be too numerous to count

EXODUS 1:15-22
Pharaoh ordered all
Hebrew boys to be killed

MATTHEW 2:13-15
Herod slaughtered children
in an attempt to kill Jesus

EXODUS 2:3
Moses was placed in
a basket in the Nile

GENESIS 6–8
The Hebrew word for "basket"
is the same word for ark used in
the story of Noah and the flood

EXODUS 2:15-21
Moses met his
wife at a well

GENESIS 24
Isaac met his wife at a well
JOHN 4:1-26
Jesus ministered to a
woman at a well

EXODUS 2:23-25

[23] After a long time, the king of Egypt died. The Israelites groaned because of their difficult labor, they cried out, and their cry for help because of the difficult labor ascended to God. [24] God heard their groaning, and God remembered his covenant with Abraham, with Isaac, and with Jacob. [25] God saw the Israelites, and God knew.

GOD HEARD

Time didn't stand still for the Israelites while Moses was away.

They continued to be enslaved, year after year.

They cried out. They groaned in their slavery.

And their cries rose to God.

In the final few verses of Exodus 2, we hear directly from the main character of Exodus. God heard the cries of His people and remembered His covenant with Abraham, Isaac, and Jacob. God heard, God saw, and God knew. He was about to send the Israelites the deliverer He had been preparing for them.

A few things are notable at this point in our story: First, the king who had been treating the Egyptians harshly had died. That means Moses would be able to return. Second, though, at this key turning point, there's no mention of Moses: only of God and of His covenant. Moses, after all, would not be a savior. He would be a human leader powerfully used by God.

God didn't choose Moses to lead His people to the Promised Land because of who Moses was; He chose Moses because of who He is: One who is faithful, One who never forgets, One who delivers on every promise He's ever made—even if it doesn't happen in the timeline we expect.

Eighty years had passed since Moses was a baby in a basket in the Nile.

In all those years, God wasn't just preparing Moses to be the leader he would become. He was continuing to weave a story of redemption and deliverance far beyond the Israelites for all of humanity.

God heard. God saw.
And God knew.

REFLECTIONS

Review the chart on page 37. Which connection is the most interesting to you?

These verses reveal God's perspective on Israel's suffering. How might verses like these help us when we're tempted to believe that God doesn't care?

Think back through the reading this week, reviewing the key points. How would you summarize the Bible reading from this week in a sentence or two?

PAUSE & LISTEN

Spend some time reflecting over the week's reading.

After a long time, the king of Egypt died. The Israelites groaned because of their difficult labor, and they cried out, and their cry for help because of the difficult labor ascended to God. God heard their groaning, and God remembered his covenant with Abraham, with Isaac, and with Jacob. God saw the Israelites, and God knew.

EXODUS 2:23-25

REFLECTION

Use these questions for personal reflection or group discussion on Exodus 1–2.

What stuck out to you most in this week's reading? What surprised you? Confused you?

What does this week's Scripture teach you about God and His character?

What does this week's Scripture teach you about humanity and our need for grace?

How does this week's Scripture point you to Jesus?

What steps of faith and obedience is God asking you to take through these Scriptures?

Spend a few moments thanking God for the promises we have in Him. Ask that we could trust them even when our circumstances are trying.

WEEK 2

DELIVERER

An ordinary man is God's
chosen instrument.

The story of Moses is about to expand far beyond one life. The events that unfold in these chapters are tales for all time.

It's not just that Moses would impact a great many Israelites and Egyptians as he followed God and grew into a leader.

Moses's experiences here—propelled by his faith—point to greater themes of deliverance and redemption. The book of Exodus offers an inside look at how God works—and how His story will continue all the way through the death and resurrection of Jesus. Here, we see a groundwork being laid that will prepare the Israelites (and us) for the redemption of humanity.

Within these pages, we also get a glimpse of God inviting humanity to join Him in accomplishing His plans. He speaks to Moses, but He also speaks through Moses.

Moses—an ordinary man—was God's chosen instrument. Yet God still conducts the orchestra, continuing to bring each part together at precisely the right time, in exactly the right way, for a powerful demonstration of His glory.

EXODUS 3:1-12

MOSES AND THE BURNING BUSH

3 Meanwhile, Moses was shepherding the flock of his father-in-law Jethro, the priest of Midian. He led the flock to the far side of the wilderness and came to Horeb, the mountain of God. ² Then the angel of the Lord appeared to him in a flame of fire within a bush. As Moses looked, he saw that the bush was on fire but was not consumed. ³ So Moses thought, "I must go over and look at this remarkable sight. Why isn't the bush burning up?"

⁴ When the Lord saw that he had gone over to look, God called out to him from the bush, "Moses, Moses!"

"Here I am," he answered.

⁵ "Do not come closer," he said. "Remove the sandals from your feet, for the place where you are standing is holy ground." ⁶ Then he continued, "I am the God of your father, the God of Abraham, the God of Isaac, and the God of Jacob." Moses hid his face because he was afraid to look at God.

⁷ Then the Lord said, "I have observed the misery of my people in Egypt, and have heard them crying out because of their oppressors. I know about their sufferings, ⁸ and I have come down to rescue them from the power of the Egyptians and to bring them from that land to a good and spacious land, a land flowing with milk and honey — the territory of the Canaanites, Hethites, Amorites, Perizzites, Hivites, and Jebusites. ⁹ So because the Israelites' cry for help has come to me, and I have also seen the way the Egyptians are oppressing them, ¹⁰ therefore, go. I am sending you to Pharaoh so that you may lead my people, the Israelites, out of Egypt."

¹¹ But Moses asked God, "Who am I that I should go to Pharaoh and that I should bring the Israelites out of Egypt?"

¹² He answered, "I will certainly be with you, and this will be the sign to you that I am the one who sent you: when you bring the people out of Egypt, you will all worship God at this mountain."

REMARKABLE SIGHT

Fire consumes. It envelops and destroys anything in its path in a powerful—and sometimes frightening—display. And yet, it also purifies and rejuvenates, allowing for new growth, even in areas that have been dormant.

While tending his father-in-law's flock in the desert, Moses had a unique experience: He saw a bush engulfed with flames, yet not burning up. The "remarkable sight" drew Moses close. God drew Moses close to speak to the burgeoning leader from the bush, calling him to rescue the Israelites from slavery.

As God spoke to Moses through the burning bush, He told Moses to remove his sandals, as he was standing on holy ground. The place God drew Moses to was not sacred on its own. God's presence made a nondescript desert place holy. God created a holy space to guide and direct Moses on the mission God was calling him to complete. A flurry of powerful statements followed about who He is and what He would do.

The God speaking in the bush was the same God Moses's ancestors worshiped (v. 6). God heard the cries of His people in Egypt (v. 7), and He was sending Moses to deliver them from Pharaoh's oppression (v. 10).

Understandably, Moses was overwhelmed (v.11). But God promised to be with Moses, and to bring him back to the very place they were standing as free and redeemed people (v. 12).

The words from the fire sparked a mission to renew Israel. It was an astonishing display of God's presence. But it was only one of many to come.

God spoke to Moses.

REFLECTIONS

List all the things God revealed to Moses about Himself in these verses. You may want to write below or go back to the previous page and underline in the portion of Scripture.

After telling Moses who He is, God gave Moses a mission. How is God's identity related to His mission?

To hear God, Moses had to listen to Him. Where are you making space to hear from God?

INSIGHT

Throughout Exodus God promises to give Israel "the territory of the Canaanites, Hethites, Amorites, Perizzites, Hivites, and Jebusites." To us, this may seem like an odd way to describe a place. However, God described it this way intentionally. It not only tells them who occupies the land currently, it also provides a way of referring to the land that would be memorable. At the time Exodus was written many of the people were not literate, so they would tell this story together out loud. Describing the land this way, over and over again, would have caused it to stick in their memory.

Moses to Jesus

Jesus is the prophet God raised up to be a better Moses.

HEBREWS 11:23-29

[23] By faith Moses, after he was born, was hidden by his parents for three months, because they saw that the child was beautiful, and they didn't fear the king's edict. [24] By faith Moses, when he had grown up, refused to be called the son of Pharaoh's daughter [25] and chose to suffer with the people of God rather than to enjoy the fleeting pleasure of sin. [26] For he considered reproach for the sake of Christ to be greater wealth than the treasures of Egypt, since he was looking ahead to the reward.

[27] By faith he left Egypt behind, not being afraid of the king's anger, for Moses persevered as one who sees him who is invisible. [28] By faith he instituted the Passover and the sprinkling of the blood, so that the destroyer of the firstborn might not touch the Israelites. [29] By faith they crossed the Red Sea as though they were on dry land. When the Egyptians attempted to do this, they were drowned.

DEUTERONOMY 18:18-19

[18] I will raise up for them a prophet like you from among their brothers. And I will put my words in his mouth, and he will tell them everything I command him. [19] I will hold accountable whoever does not listen to my words that he speaks in my name.

Moses

Humble
NUMBERS 12:3

A faithful servant
NUMBERS 12:7

Spoke to God face to face
EXODUS 33:11

*Had to veil his face after
speaking with God*
EXODUS 34:29-35

An unsurpassed prophet
DEUTERONOMY 34:10-12

Represented the people to God
EXODUS 20:19

*The mediator of
the old covenant*
EXODUS 24:8

Jesus

Humble
PHILIPPIANS 2:5-8

A faithful Son
HEBREWS 3:1-6

The visible glory of God
2 CORINTHIANS 4:6; HEBREWS 1:1-3

*Removes the veil so that
we can see God*
2 CORINTHIANS 3:13-18

The promised prophet
DEUTERONOMY 18:18-19

Represented God to people
1 TIMOTHY 2:5-6

*The mediator of the
new covenant*
HEBREWS 9:15

EXODUS 3:13-22

[13] Then Moses asked God, "If I go to the Israelites and say to them, 'The God of your ancestors has sent me to you,' and they ask me, 'What is his name?' what should I tell them?"

[14] God replied to Moses, "I AM WHO I AM. This is what you are to say to the Israelites: I AM has sent me to you." [15] God also said to Moses, "Say this to the Israelites: The LORD, the God of your ancestors, the God of Abraham, the God of Isaac, and the God of Jacob, has sent me to you. This is my name forever; this is how I am to be remembered in every generation.

[16] "Go and assemble the elders of Israel and say to them: The LORD, the God of your ancestors, the God of Abraham, Isaac, and Jacob, has appeared to me and said: I have paid close attention to you and to what has been done to you in Egypt. [17] And I have promised you that I will bring you up from the misery of Egypt to the land of the Canaanites, Hethites, Amorites, Perizzites, Hivites, and Jebusites — a land flowing with milk and honey. [18] They will listen to what you say. Then you, along with the elders of Israel, must go to the king of Egypt and say to him: The LORD, the God of the Hebrews, has met with us. Now please let us go on a three-day trip into the wilderness so that we may sacrifice to the LORD our God.

[19] "However, I know that the king of Egypt will not allow you to go, even under force from a strong hand. [20] But when I stretch out my hand and strike Egypt with all my miracles that I will perform in it, after that, he will let you go. [21] And I will give these people such favor with the Egyptians that when you go, you will not go empty-handed. [22] Each woman will ask her neighbor and any woman staying in her house for silver and gold jewelry, and clothing, and you will put them on your sons and daughters. So you will plunder the Egyptians."

WHAT'S IN A NAME?

Moses was in the middle of a direct conversation with the Creator of the universe—One who promised to be with him for the mission ahead—and he had a reasonable question—*If I go to the Israelites and tell them You sent me, what if they ask who You are?*

Surely, the question came with trepidation. We can almost hear the underlying question Moses was asking: *What if all they see is me?*

God answered in a surprising way. He didn't bolster Moses by commenting on his character traits or strengths; rather, God focused on Himself, beginning with His name—I AM WHO I AM. In His name God was saying, I am eternal, limitless, creator of all that exists. His name defines who He is.

As God continued speaking to Moses, every phrase pointed back to His identity, power, and promises. For us focusing on ourselves is selfish, for God it is natural. Because who else would God praise? He alone is without equal.

Moses was full of doubt and concerns and was searching for certainty. Like all of us, Moses didn't understand the story wasn't about him. The story of Exodus doesn't only involve Moses, the story is ultimately about God.

God's deliverance was not dependent on Moses's or anyone else's ability. He used Moses—just as He can use any one of us—to accomplish His purposes. It requires only that we keep our eyes on who God is and be willing to do what God asks. Deliverance depends on the work of God, not the quality or confidence of God's servants.

God revealed His name to Moses.

REFLECTIONS

What did God promise to do through Moses? Why is it important to recognize God is working through Moses?

Moses offered numerous excuses to keep from following God's plan. What excuses do we offer?

God answered Moses's doubts by leading Moses to focus on His identity. Spend a few moments rereading this passage focusing on who God is. Write down a phrase that summarizes your thoughts.

INSIGHTS

Remember from last week, the Hebrew title of Exodus is *Names.* When names are revealed to us in this book, it is significant. In these verses, we learn the personal name of the God of the whole world—I AM. In Hebrew this word is *Yaweh.* To Jews, this name was so holy that they would not say it out loud. As you read the Bible every time you see a capital LORD, it's the word *Yaweh.*

EXODUS 4:1-9

MIRACULOUS SIGNS FOR MOSES

4 Moses answered, "What if they won't believe me and will not obey me but say, 'The Lᴏʀᴅ did not appear to you'?"

² The Lᴏʀᴅ asked him, "What is that in your hand?"

"A staff," he replied.

³ "Throw it on the ground," he said. So Moses threw it on the ground, it became a snake, and he ran from it. ⁴ The Lᴏʀᴅ told Moses, "Stretch out your hand and grab it by the tail." So he stretched out his hand and caught it, and it became a staff in his hand. ⁵ "This will take place," he continued, "so that they will believe that the Lᴏʀᴅ, the God of their ancestors, the God of Abraham, the God of Isaac, and the God of Jacob, has appeared to you."

⁶ In addition the Lᴏʀᴅ said to him, "Put your hand inside your cloak." So he put his hand inside his cloak, and when he took it out, his hand was diseased, resembling snow. ⁷ "Put your hand back inside your cloak," he said. So he put his hand back inside his cloak, and when he took it out, it had again become like the rest of his skin. ⁸ "If they will not believe you and will not respond to the evidence of the first sign, they may believe the evidence of the second sign. ⁹ And if they don't believe even these two signs or listen to what you say, take some water from the Nile and pour it on the dry ground. The water you take from the Nile will become blood on the ground."

SIGNS

Moses heard God lay out a specific plan to bring the Israelites out of slavery. God promised they would leave the cramped and oppressive landscape of Egypt and enter a land that was open and fertile and filled with everything that they needed.

It was a big plan. An extraordinary strategy. And yet, God chose to use an ordinary man. More than that, God used ordinary means.

God asked Moses what he held in his hand. It was a staff—a common instrument used by any shepherd. Yet God was about to use it in a miraculous way.

God told Moses to throw the staff onto the ground, and it turned into a snake. Moses was so shocked by this that he ran (v. 3). When Moses grabbed it by the tail, the snake became a staff once again. God followed that with two more signs—turning Moses's skin white with leprosy and turning water into blood. These miraculous displays weren't just for Moses. God gave Moses these signs so that all who saw them would know that they were from God.

Throughout Exodus, God used the staff of Moses as a conduit to reveal His power and show His authority. When we ask God for a sign, sometimes He'll say yes. However, much more often, God will take something ordinary, like our circumstances and our willingness to do what He says, and use those things to help the people around us see who God is and what He is like.

Moses's ordinary obedience was as important as the miraculous signs God gave him. Without obedience, the signs wouldn't have been displayed. We might not expect to have the same kind of signs Moses had, but we can follow God in obedience.

God equipped Moses with powerful signs.

REFLECTIONS

When have you asked God to work in a specific way so that you'll know it's Him?

Why do we long for signs from God?

What is an ordinary step of obedience you can take today to walk closer with God?

EXODUS 4:10-17

¹⁰ But Moses replied to the Lord, "Please, Lord, I have never been eloquent — either in the past or recently or since you have been speaking to your servant — because my mouth and my tongue are sluggish."

¹¹ The Lord said to him, "Who placed a mouth on humans? Who makes a person mute or deaf, seeing or blind? Is it not I, the Lord? ¹² Now go! I will help you speak and I will teach you what to say."

¹³ Moses said, "Please, Lord, send someone else."

¹⁴ Then the Lord's anger burned against Moses, and he said, "Isn't Aaron the Levite your brother? I know that he can speak well. And also, he is on his way now to meet you. He will rejoice when he sees you. ¹⁵ You will speak with him and tell him what to say. I will help both you and him to speak and will teach you both what to do. ¹⁶ He will speak to the people for you. He will serve as a mouth for you, and you will serve as God to him. ¹⁷ And take this staff in your hand that you will perform the signs with."

CONFIRMATION

God shared His plan with Moses and worked through Moses's doubts. Moses continued to bring His insecurity before God. Despite God telling Moses he would have all he needed, Moses found trusting God difficult. Once again, God pointed to His power rather than Moses's circumstances.

He heard Moses's concerns and was willing to address them. God had already prepared his brother, Aaron, to share the load. The Bible tells us that Aaron was already on his way. Aaron had grown into a man good with words, one able to fill the gap for Moses's insecurities about public speaking. God set a plan in place. Moses would speak to Aaron and Aaron would proclaim God's words to Pharaoh. God promised to help them.

It's not the only time we see God confirming His plan by bringing together the right people—and the right preparations—at the right time. The daughter of Pharaoh just happened to be the first person to see Moses floating as a baby in the river. When our circumstances seem overwhelming and overpowering, God is still more powerful than our circumstances.

God knows what's coming. He knows what we need and is willing to help us when our hearts grow faint and our nerves fail us.

God gave Moses support.

REFLECTIONS

What excuses did Moses offer to God?

Why might God send Moses someone who had the skills Moses lacked, rather than just supernaturally "fixing" Moses? What does it mean to you to know that God is willing to meet you in moments of insecurity and uncertainty?

What support has God given you to follow and obey Him?

I am.

In John 8, Jesus found Himself in a dispute with Jewish leaders where He makes the argument that Abraham, the Jewish patriarch, "rejoiced to see my day; he saw it and was glad" (John 8:56). Astounded by this statement, the Jews wonder how Jesus could've seen Abraham, who had been dead for centuries. Jesus replied, "Truly I tell you, before Abraham was, I am" (v. 58). In saying this, Jesus was intentionally linking Himself to the personal name of God. We know the Jews understood His reference because they sought stones to kill Him for blasphemy.

Throughout John, Jesus makes several intentional I AM statements:

"I am the bread of life."

JOHN 6:35. Jesus is the one who satisfies spiritual hunger.

"I am the light of the world."

JOHN 8:12. Jesus overwhelms and overcomes sin and darkness.

"I am the gate for the sheep."

JOHN 10:7. Jesus protects His followers from those who would harm them.

"I am the good shepherd."

JOHN 10:11. Jesus cares for and watches over His followers.

"I am the resurrection and the life."

JOHN 11:25. Jesus brings and gives eternal life.

"I am the way, the truth, and the life."

JOHN 14:6. Jesus is the source of knowledge about God.

"I am the true vine."

JOHN 15:1. Jesus connects His followers to spiritual vitality.

EXODUS 4:18-23, 27-31

MOSES'S RETURN TO EGYPT

¹⁸ Then Moses went back to his father-in-law, Jethro, and said to him, "Please let me return to my relatives in Egypt and see if they are still living."

Jethro said to Moses, "Go in peace."

¹⁹ Now in Midian the Lord told Moses, "Return to Egypt, for all the men who wanted to kill you are dead." ²⁰ So Moses took his wife and sons, put them on a donkey, and returned to the land of Egypt. And Moses took God's staff in his hand.

²¹ The Lord instructed Moses, "When you go back to Egypt, make sure you do before Pharaoh all the wonders that I have put within your power. But I will harden his heart so that he won't let the people go. ²² And you will say to Pharaoh: This is what the Lord says: Israel is my firstborn son. ²³ I told you: Let my son go so that he may worship me, but you refused to let him go. Look, I am about to kill your firstborn son!"

————

REUNION OF MOSES AND AARON

²⁷ Now the Lord had said to Aaron, "Go and meet Moses in the wilderness." So he went and met him at the mountain of God and kissed him. ²⁸ Moses told Aaron everything the Lord had sent him to say, and about all the signs he had commanded him to do. ²⁹ Then Moses and Aaron went and assembled all the elders of the Israelites. ³⁰ Aaron repeated everything the Lord had said to Moses and performed the signs before the people. ³¹ The people believed, and when they heard that the Lord had paid attention to them and that he had seen their misery, they knelt low and worshiped.

PREPARED

Moses was on the move. Questions answered, encouragement provided, promises made: He was returning to Egypt. Prepared.

We find him telling his father-in-law that he must return to Egypt to find his people. He set out with his wife, his sons, and his staff in hand. God had urged Moses to perform all the wonders that He had given him the power to do, but He also offered a warning: The Pharaoh will be stubborn. His heart will be hardened.

Pharaoh's refusal to release the Israelites from slavery would allow God's full power and glory to be revealed. God works in ways we might not understand but that always show who He is. Everything God does is intentional.

Moses spent forty years in Midian away from his first home in Egypt. God used all that time to shape Moses into the deliverer of Israel. In chapter 2 we read that God saw, God heard, and God knew about the struggle of His people. He also intervened. He sought and prepared a man who would be instrumental in leading the people out of Egypt.

Just because God asks us to do something doesn't mean it will be easy. Just because He's with us doesn't mean that all will recognize what He is trying to accomplish. We will have what we need. Moses had been prepared and given all he needed to be God's servant. He returned to Egypt to unfold God's plan of redemption.

When the people of Israel heard the Lord's plan, they believed what they heard, knew that the Lord cared about them, and worshiped Him in response. God had prepared a plan. It was about to unfold.

Moses returned to Egypt, prepared.

REFLECTIONS

Think back over the last two weeks in Exodus. What did God do to prepare Moses for this moment?

In verse 31, the people heard God's plans, believed God's plans, and worshiped Him in response. What has God done in your life recently that you can pause and worship Him for?

God is at work in your life, just as He was at work in Moses's life. What might God be preparing you for?

DAY

13

PAUSE & LISTEN
Spend some time reflecting over the week's reading.

The people believed, and when they heard that the LORD had paid attention to them and that he had seen their misery, they knelt low and worshiped.

EXODUS 4:31

REFLECTION
Use these questions for personal reflection or group discussion on Exodus 3–4.

What stuck out to you most in this week's reading? What surprised you? Confused you?

What does this week's Scripture teach you about God and His character?

What does this week's Scripture teach you about humanity and our need for grace?

How does this week's Scripture point you to Jesus?

What steps of faith and obedience is God asking you to take through these Scriptures?

PRAY

Spend a few moments reflecting on God's character from the reading this week. Pray that as a result of reading this week that we would love and trust Him more.

WEEK 3

DISCOURAGEMENT

God is often at work in ways
we don't recognize.

Those who say that the first step of any journey is the hardest haven't traveled very far. It's not the first step. It's the 56th. The 348th. The 5,929th, when it still feels like no progress has been made.

God called Moses to stand before Pharaoh on His behalf. But it was not a one-and-done experience. Moses appeared before Pharaoh time and time again with stern warnings and assurances of consequences.

Before things got better for the people Moses wanted to help, they had to get worse.

The Israelites had been enslaved for years. They longed for freedom and escape from servitude. They longed to see God at work on their behalf, righting the injustice they endured. But they wouldn't see it yet.

Exodus teaches God is often at work in ways we don't recognize. As the Israelites kept laboring day after day, as discouragement and exhaustion continued to creep in, God continued working behind the scenes. The songs of Israel remind us:

> Indeed, the Protector of Israel
> does not slumber or sleep.
> **PSALMS 121:4**

How did Israel respond? How will we?

EXODUS 5:1-9

MOSES CONFRONTS PHARAOH

5 Later, Moses and Aaron went in and said to Pharaoh, "This is what the LORD, the God of Israel, says: Let my people go, so that they may hold a festival for me in the wilderness."

² But Pharaoh responded, "Who is the LORD that I should obey him by letting Israel go? I don't know the LORD, and besides, I will not let Israel go."

³ They answered, "The God of the Hebrews has met with us. Please let us go on a three-day trip into the wilderness so that we may sacrifice to the LORD our God, or else he may strike us with plague or sword."

⁴ The king of Egypt said to them, "Moses and Aaron, why are you causing the people to neglect their work? Get to your labor!" ⁵ Pharaoh also said, "Look, the people of the land are so numerous, and you would stop them from their labor."

FURTHER OPPRESSION OF ISRAEL

⁶ That day Pharaoh commanded the overseers of the people as well as their foremen, ⁷ "Don't continue to supply the people with straw for making bricks, as before. They must go and gather straw for themselves. ⁸ But require the same quota of bricks from them as they were making before; do not reduce it. For they are slackers — that is why they are crying out, 'Let us go and sacrifice to our God.' ⁹ Impose heavier work on the men. Then they will be occupied with it and not pay attention to deceptive words."

REJECTION

Last week's reading ended with the people of Israel worshiping in response to God sending them a deliverer. This week begins with the first of many conversations between Moses and Pharaoh. Moses, with Aaron by his side, headed straight to Pharaoh to request what the Lord, the God of Israel, had told them to say: "Let my people go."

There's only one problem: Pharaoh didn't know this God. He had no respect for God's power—or for these brothers, Moses and Aaron.

Pharaoh, then, didn't just say no to God's request. He also increased the workload of the Israelites, making their already challenging situation even more so.

The scenario was playing out exactly as God said it would, including Pharaoh's stubbornness. Thankfully, Pharaoh was not in charge. God was, and He prepared Moses for this situation.

This preview confirmed that God's plan for the Israelites would work out as He said. He promised that He would deliver the people from their misery and take them to a land flowing with milk and honey—a place of abundance, blessing, and beauty. However, the path was not be straight; there was still much ground to cover—and much more for God to accomplish through His servant, Moses. According to what He said.

When our lives become complex and confusing and nothing works as we had hoped, we can hold fast to what God has said, and who He is. He will always be faithful, even (or perhaps especially) when our circumstances seem overwhelming.

God's plan would proceed as He said.

REFLECTIONS

What reasons did Pharaoh give for rejecting God's request through Moses?

Though things went exactly as God had said, the Israelites lives still became harder. How do we cultivate faith in who God is so that we can trust what He said when things don't go as well as we hoped?

How should we respond when our faith in God complicates our lives or makes them more difficult?

INSIGHT

When Moses and Aaron were negotiating with Pharaoh, their goal was to be released from slavery, but they began by asking to hold a festival in the wilderness. It may seem odd to us that they just didn't come right out and say what they wanted to begin with. This was actually an ancient negotiating tactic where parties expressed their wishes incrementally.

EXODUS 5:10-18

10 So the overseers and foremen of the people went out and said to them, "This is what Pharaoh says: 'I am not giving you straw. 11 Go get straw yourselves wherever you can find it, but there will be no reduction at all in your workload.'" 12 So the people scattered throughout the land of Egypt to gather stubble for straw. 13 The overseers insisted, "Finish your assigned work each day, just as you did when straw was provided." 14 Then the Israelite foremen, whom Pharaoh's slave drivers had set over the people, were beaten and asked, "Why haven't you finished making your prescribed number of bricks yesterday or today, as you did before?"

15 So the Israelite foremen went in and cried for help to Pharaoh: "Why are you treating your servants this way? 16 No straw has been given to your servants, yet they say to us, 'Make bricks!' Look, your servants are being beaten, but it is your own people who are at fault."

17 But he said, "You are slackers. Slackers! That is why you are saying, 'Let us go sacrifice to the Lord.' 18 Now get to work. No straw will be given to you, but you must produce the same quantity of bricks."

THE COST

In our ongoing story, Moses had an advantage Pharaoh wasn't aware of and didn't fully appreciate. Though it seemed like Pharaoh had all the power and resources, Moses represented the true God with truly unlimited power and resources. Moses was encouraged and commissioned by God through the burning bush. He heard God call him by name.

Moses and Aaron met with the elders of Israel before they met with Pharaoh. They told the leaders everything God had said, and Moses performed the miraculous signs. They, too, believed. The Israelites bowed down in worship.

But what about now?

All they knew was that the workload had increased. In addition to making bricks, the Israelites needed to find their own straw. The labor was backbreaking. Their foremen were beaten.

The hard truth is that sometimes our obedience makes things worse for us—or for others. But the Bible tells us in the book of Romans that God works all things for the good of those who love Him (8:28). If that's true (and it is) then there must be deeper reasons for what He has called us to do.

This theme in Exodus shows up in many other places in the Bible. The Scriptures are filled with examples of situations that looked increasingly dark before the light finally appeared. Including, of course, the days that Jesus lay dead before His resurrection.

Obedience is indeed costly, for us and those around us. But obedience is the way we say yes to God's plan for our lives. We cannot follow God without obeying Him. And over time, obedience builds our ability to trust God and His plans for our lives.

But Pharaoh would resist.

REFLECTIONS

When the Israelite foremen were beaten for not delivering the required number of bricks, they cried out to Pharaoh instead of crying out to God. Why do you think they did this?

When have you looked to someone or something other than God to deliver you?

How does being familiar with stories like this one, where pain leads to God's plan, help us trust God when we might not understand?

CONNECTING THE STORY

The Bible is filled with God working in seemingly hopeless situations. David was anointed king, but then fled for his life. Jeremiah was ridiculed for speaking God's word. Daniel was thrown to the lions. Nehemiah was opposed as he sought to repair the walls of Jerusalem. Jesus was crucified. The apostle James was murdered. The apostle John was exiled. The apostle Paul was beaten. And yet God was at work during their suffering. All these servants of God knew the stories of how God redeemed His struggling people.

EXODUS 5:19-23

[19] The Israelite foremen saw that they were in trouble when they were told, "You cannot reduce your daily quota of bricks." [20] When they left Pharaoh, they confronted Moses and Aaron, who stood waiting to meet them.

[21] "May the LORD take note of you and judge," they said to them, "because you have made us reek to Pharaoh and his officials — putting a sword in their hand to kill us!"

[22] So Moses went back to the LORD and asked, "Lord, why have you caused trouble for this people? And why did you ever send me? [23] Ever since I went in to Pharaoh to speak in your name he has caused trouble for this people, and you haven't rescued your people at all."

ANGER

Things went from bad to worse; blame was quick to spread. The Israelite foremen, caught between the demands of Pharaoh and the complaints of the workers, set their sights on Moses. They asked God to judge Moses.

When the foremen were oppressed by Pharaoh, they turned to Pharaoh—not God—to get relief. In their desperation, they went to the wrong source. Now in their anger, they turned to the wrong source again. Their anger was misplaced.

Moses recognized the source of their hardship. He turned to God and asked sharp questions that might surprise us, but Moses's anger was also a cry of faith.

To doubt God or be angry at Him, you first have to believe that He exists and can do something about your situation; if not there would be no reason to be angry. The Bible is full of people who burn with anger and frustration at God. Often it's because they haven't seen Him deliver on His promises—at least not yet. Jeremiah was angry with God. David was angry with God. Jonah. Job.

It's easy to believe God when His work is apparent, and when He seems to be hearing and answering our prayers, isn't it? But it's the times in between that call for greater faith, patience, and perseverance.

Day after day, the Israelites were faced with hard labor, and the foremen were being asked to make it harder still.

Day after day, they were called to believe that God would hold true to His promises, and that He would deliver them. But when?

God is able to withstand our anger. It will not thwart or delay His faithfulness.

Moses cried out to God for relief.

REFLECTIONS

Why was Moses's cry of frustration also an act of faith?

Do you feel the freedom to be frustrated with God? Why or why not?

Read Psalm 77. What would it look like for you to pray a prayer like this? When have you needed to?

6 But the Lord replied to Moses, "Now you will see what I will do to Pharaoh: because of a strong hand he will let them go, and because of a strong hand he will drive them from his land."

GOD PROMISES FREEDOM

² Then God spoke to Moses, telling him, "I am the Lord. ³ I appeared to Abraham, Isaac, and Jacob as God Almighty, but I was not known to them by my name 'the Lord.' ⁴ I also established my covenant with them to give them the land of Canaan, the land they lived in as aliens. ⁵ Furthermore, I have heard the groaning of the Israelites, whom the Egyptians are forcing to work as slaves, and I have remembered my covenant.

⁶ "Therefore tell the Israelites: I am the Lord, and I will bring you out from the forced labor of the Egyptians and rescue you from slavery to them. I will redeem you with an outstretched arm and great acts of judgment. ⁷ I will take you as my people, and I will be your God. You will know that I am the Lord your God, who brought you out from the forced labor of the Egyptians. ⁸ I will bring you to the land that I swore to give to Abraham, Isaac, and Jacob, and I will give it to you as a possession. I am the Lord." ⁹ Moses told this to the Israelites, but they did not listen to him because of their broken spirit and hard labor.

¹⁰ Then the Lord spoke to Moses, ¹¹ "Go and tell Pharaoh king of Egypt to let the Israelites go from his land."

¹² But Moses said in the Lord's presence, "If the Israelites will not listen to me, then how will Pharaoh listen to me, since I am such a poor speaker?" ¹³ Then the Lord spoke to Moses and Aaron and gave them commands concerning both the Israelites and Pharaoh king of Egypt to bring the Israelites out of the land of Egypt.

CALL TO ME

Later in the story of Scripture, many years beyond the events of Exodus, when God's people the Israelites have been an established nation, God spoke through the prophet Jeremiah saying, "Call to me and I will answer you and tell you great and incomprehensible things you do not know" (Jeremiah 33:3). God is not like us. He is unchanging, so this promise that was true in Jeremiah's day was also true in Moses's day. If God's people call to Him, He will answer.

Moses knew this firsthand. No surprise, then, that we find him here again: calling out to God and receiving reassurance in return.

God promised Moses once again that Pharaoh would release the Israelites from their slavery. He reminded Moses of who He is, and of His covenant with Abraham, Isaac, and Jacob. Those promises God gave to those people still applied to Moses and the Israelites he was tasked with leading.

Moses conveyed all this to the Israelites, hoping to pass on the encouragement and assurance of salvation. But the Israelites were too beaten down to hear or believe him.

Moses's anguish was real—if his own people wouldn't listen, why would Pharaoh?

Sometimes God will ask us to stand in faith before those who don't see things the way we do. In those moments, it's natural to question our own abilities. Remember, though, that God didn't call Moses because of who Moses was; He called him because of who He is—and who He will be for all time.

His covenant and promises continue to stand. They are more powerful and dependable than any strength or ability we might bring to the table.

God received Moses's cry.

REFLECTIONS

When Moses cried out to God, what reasons did He give Moses to trust Him?

Look again at verse 9. The Israelites could not receive God's comfort because of "their broken spirit and hard labor." How can pain and exhaustion keep us from hearing God?

The people's response gave Moses a crisis of confidence. How can we learn to trust what God has said about us rather than how people respond?

Covenants

In Exodus God is moved to act on Israel's behalf because of the covenant that He made with Abraham. A covenant is a chosen and binding relationship where two parties commit to support one another towards a goal. Covenants create a formal relationship with expectations for each side. The most common covenant in our culture today is marriage. Throughout the Bible there are five major covenants between people and God.

The Covenant with Noah

GENESIS 8:20-9:17. God made an unconditional promise to never again destroy the world through a flood like He did in the days of Noah. The rainbow was a sign of this covenant.

The Covenant with Abraham

GENESIS 12, 15, AND 17. God promised to bless Abraham with children, give his descendants a specific land on which to live (the Promised Land), and bless the whole world through Abraham's offspring. The sign for this covenant was circumcision.

The Covenant with Moses

EXODUS 19-24. After God rescued Israel from Egypt to make them a great nation and fulfill His promise to Abraham, He made a covenant with Moses and Israel by giving them a group of commandments to follow. The Israelites would find blessings if they obeyed and hardship if they disobeyed. The sign for this covenant was a day of rest (the Sabbath).

The Covenant with David

2 SAMUEL 7. God made a promise to David that a descendant from his line would rule forever over the house of Israel. God called Israel to be faithful, but promised to fulfill the promise whether they were faithful or not. Unlike the other covenants, this one had no sign.

The New Covenant

JEREMIAH 31:31-34; EZEKIEL 36:22-32; LUKE 22:19-22. God made an unconditional promise to give people who follow Him a new heart by placing His Spirit inside of them. This covenant was promised by the prophets but fulfilled in Jesus. The sign for this covenant is the Lord's Supper which Christians celebrate together to remember Jesus's death and proclaim it until He returns.

EXODUS 7:1-6

7 The Lord answered Moses, "See, I have made you like God to Pharaoh, and Aaron your brother will be your prophet. [2] You must say whatever I command you; then Aaron your brother must declare it to Pharaoh so that he will let the Israelites go from his land. [3] But I will harden Pharaoh's heart and multiply my signs and wonders in the land of Egypt. [4] Pharaoh will not listen to you, but I will put my hand into Egypt and bring the military divisions of my people the Israelites out of the land of Egypt by great acts of judgment. [5] The Egyptians will know that I am the Lord when I stretch out my hand against Egypt and bring out the Israelites from among them."

[6] So Moses and Aaron did this; they did just as the Lord commanded them.

AS THE LORD COMMANDED

Having wrestled with his own doubts and the doubts of his people, Moses was about to head into a familiar setting for him—a direct confrontation with Pharaoh.

Moses and Aaron were still in the early days of their dance with Pharaoh. We may wonder, as we follow along, why the steps are so many—and why the moves are so complex. But not God. He is in control of every detail. He continues to keep time.

He is the Lord of the dance. Everything God promises will come to pass. In these verses, God promised Moses that He was about to act in such a clear and powerful way that everyone in Egypt would know that He was God.

He would do this when He stretched His hand out against Egypt and brought the Israelites out. All Moses had to do was obey. And he did.

We finally read in verse 6, "So Moses and Aaron did this; they did just as the Lord commanded them."

Moses set aside his questions and doubts. He embraced God's plan and direction on his life. He chose to obey and watch God work.

The scene God described to Moses happened again and again throughout Exodus. Moses asked for freedom. Pharaoh refused. God performed miracles. Pharaoh relented, then hardened his heart. Then the steps began again. Yet each time, Moses was faithful to do as God asked, and God was faithful to do what He said.

Moses and Aaron did just as the Lord said.

REFLECTIONS

Consider all that Moses had seen. This time he obeyed without complaint or resistance. What led Moses to this point?

When has obeying God been more of a process than a straight line for you?

If obedience is more of a process right now, what is the next small step you need to take?

PAUSE & LISTEN

Spend some time reflecting over the week's reading.

"The Egyptians will know that I am the LORD when I stretch out my hand against Egypt and bring out the Israelites from among them." So Moses and Aaron did this; they did just as the LORD commanded them. Moses was eighty years old and Aaron eighty-three when they spoke to Pharaoh.

EXODUS 7:5–7

REFLECTION

Use these questions for personal reflection or group discussion on Exodus 5:1–7:6.

What stuck out to you most in this week's reading? What surprised you? Confused you?

What does this week's Scripture teach you about God and His character?

What does this week's Scripture teach you about humanity and our need for grace?

How does this week's Scripture point you to Jesus?

What steps of faith and obedience is God asking you to take through these Scriptures?

PRAY

Spend a few moments praying for those you know who are struggling or discouraged.
Ask God to move on their behalf.

WEEK 4

POWER

God will not be thwarted.

Scripture is full of stories that bring awe, wonder—and questions—to the reader. No doubt it was the same for those who lived them out.

God demonstrated His power through ten intense plagues, each one a challenge to the numerous gods that the Egyptians worshiped. Egypt and her people were plagued by frogs, locusts, hail, death, darkness, and more. And through them all, Pharaoh's heart remained hardened. He did not yet let the Israelites go.

The escalating afflictions raised the stakes for God to show His power and deliverance. Pharaoh's own magicians attempted to keep up with their own tricks but didn't succeed for long. It was not until the tenth plague that Pharaoh finally relented. Even then, we don't see the end of the story.

God must tear down before He will rebuild. He must conquer sin and evil before He can establish His ways.

Take note of a couple of things as you read this week: First, the plagues God brought affected the Egyptians and the Israelites in different ways. And second, Pharaoh's sorcerers attempted to disprove the miracles of God by replicating them. In some cases, they were able to bring about the same results. One thing they were not able to do though was reverse anything that God did. He cannot be thwarted, and His displays of power and presence will stand.

EXODUS 7:14-25

THE FIRST PLAGUE: WATER TURNED TO BLOOD

¹⁴ Then the Lord said to Moses, "Pharaoh's heart is hard: He refuses to let the people go. ¹⁵ Go to Pharaoh in the morning. When you see him walking out to the water, stand ready to meet him by the bank of the Nile. Take in your hand the staff that turned into a snake. ¹⁶ Tell him: The Lord, the God of the Hebrews, has sent me to tell you: Let my people go, so that they may worship me in the wilderness. But so far you have not listened. ¹⁷ This is what the Lord says: Here is how you will know that I am the Lord. Watch. I am about to strike the water in the Nile with the staff in my hand, and it will turn to blood. ¹⁸ The fish in the Nile will die, the river will stink, and the Egyptians will be unable to drink water from it."

¹⁹ So the Lord said to Moses, "Tell Aaron: Take your staff and stretch out your hand over the waters of Egypt — over their rivers, canals, ponds, and all their water reservoirs — and they will become blood. There will be blood throughout the land of Egypt, even in wooden and stone containers."

²⁰ Moses and Aaron did just as the Lord had commanded; in the sight of Pharaoh and his officials, he raised the staff and struck the water in the Nile, and all the water in the Nile was turned to blood. ²¹ The fish in the Nile died, and the river smelled so bad the Egyptians could not drink water from it. There was blood throughout the land of Egypt.

²² But the magicians of Egypt did the same thing by their occult practices. So Pharaoh's heart was hard, and he would not listen to them, as the Lord had said. ²³ Pharaoh turned around, went into his palace, and didn't take even this to heart. ²⁴ All the Egyptians dug around the Nile for water to drink because they could not drink the water from the river. ²⁵ Seven days passed after the Lord struck the Nile.

LIFEBLOOD

The first plague to hit Egypt landed a direct blow. While Pharaoh and his officials stood by, Moses struck the Nile with his staff, and the water turned to blood. For seven days, the water was foul and red; the fish died. Even the water stored in pots and bowls turned. Aaron stretched his hand over the streams, canals, and other bodies of water in Egypt, and they too turned to blood.

Here is how you will know that I am the Lord. Watch (v. 17).

Blood holds the power of life and death. In the Bible, blood is consistently tied to atonement, sacrifice, and consecration.

For the Egyptians, the Nile was the source of life. It was inextricably linked to Egypt's fertility and prosperity. The river was so revered that it was considered a manifestation of a god all its own, the "Father of Life" and "Mother of All Men." A strike on the Nile was a direct assault on the Egyptians' way of life.

The Nile defined Egyptian culture: Its waters helped provide fertile soil for food, water to drink, delivery of resources, travel, and trade with other nations. The Egyptians based their calendar on when it would flood, so they'd know when to plant and when to harvest.

The Nile, the longest river in the world, stretching more than 4,000 miles, loomed large in the eyes of the Egyptians.

God loomed larger. He stretched out His hands and made the source of Egyptian life and livelihood lifeless. And yet Pharaoh's heart was so hard he ignored the plain work of God right in front of him, content to trust the deception of his magicians. But God's work became harder and harder to deny.

Rivers turned to blood.

REFLECTIONS

What did God direct Moses and Aaron to do in this passage? What did this plague demonstrate about God's power?

This passage begins and ends with statements about Pharaoh's heart. What does this tell us about the king of Egypt?

Why are we willing to dismiss God's work and power in favor of "easy" explanations like Pharaoh did with the Egyptians?

INSIGHT

The word for *hard* used to describe Pharaoh's heart means "heavy." In Egyptian culture, they believed that when a ruler died their heart would be weighed in the afterlife. If their heart was found to be heavier than a feather, they would be devoured. Only God can cleanse and lighten the burden in our hearts, and Pharaoh rejected Him at every opportunity.

EXODUS 8:20-32

THE FOURTH PLAGUE: SWARMS OF FLIES

20 The LORD said to Moses, "Get up early in the morning and present yourself to Pharaoh when you see him going out to the water. Tell him: This is what the LORD says: Let my people go, so that they may worship me. 21 But if you will not let my people go, then I will send swarms of flies against you, your officials, your people, and your houses. The Egyptians' houses will swarm with flies, and so will the land where they live. 22 But on that day I will give special treatment to the land of Goshen, where my people are living; no flies will be there. This way you will know that I, the LORD, am in the land. 23 I will make a distinction between my people and your people. This sign will take place tomorrow."

24 And the LORD did this. Thick swarms of flies went into Pharaoh's palace and his officials' houses. Throughout Egypt the land was ruined because of the swarms of flies. 25 Then Pharaoh summoned Moses and Aaron and said, "Go sacrifice to your God within the country."

26 But Moses said, "It would not be right to do that, because what we will sacrifice to the LORD our God is detestable to the Egyptians. If we sacrifice what the Egyptians detest in front of them, won't they stone us? 27 We must go a distance of three days into the wilderness and sacrifice to the LORD our God as he instructs us."

28 Pharaoh responded, "I will let you go and sacrifice to the LORD your God in the wilderness, but don't go very far. Make an appeal for me."

29 "As soon as I leave you," Moses said, "I will appeal to the LORD, and tomorrow the swarms of flies will depart from Pharaoh, his officials, and his people. But Pharaoh must not act deceptively again by refusing to let the people go and sacrifice to the LORD." 30 Then Moses left Pharaoh's presence and appealed to the LORD. 31 The LORD did as Moses had said: He removed the swarms of flies from Pharaoh, his officials, and his people; not one was left. 32 But Pharaoh hardened his heart this time also and did not let the people go.

SEPARATION

The plagues continued. Frogs followed and then gnats. Each time, Moses and Aaron followed God's direction and warned of the impending consequences. The promised afflictions came. Pharaoh relented to make them stop, but then refused—again and again—to release the Israelites.

God then told Moses to go to Pharaoh and stand in his way as he went down to the river. Another plague would follow, but this time something was different: the flies would affect only the Egyptians, not Goshen—the area where the Hebrews lived. God promised to make a clear distinction between His people and Pharaoh's.

The following day, it happened just as expected. Swarms of flies overran Pharaoh's palace and the houses of his servants. All over Egypt, the Scriptures tell us, the land was thrown into chaos, destroyed by the flies.

What must it have been like for the Egyptians and Hebrews to notice the difference? Pharaoh—who was worshiped like a god—was unable to protect his people. The Egyptians experienced the weakness of their protector with every buzzing insect.

And how did it feel to be on the other side of the equation, seeing the hand of God's protection and deliverance?

God made a clear point—to the Egyptians and the Israelites. He and Pharaoh were not equals. Pharaoh and the gods of Egypt were powerless against the God of Israel.

This should've been evident to Pharaoh when he sought relief and Moses was able to grant it. Yet, when Pharaoh received relief, his heart was hardened once again—a familiar pattern.

Cities overrun with flies.

REFLECTIONS

Where do we see the big theme of deliverance in the way that God dealt with the Egyptians and the Israelites?

When Pharaoh received relief from the flies, he decided against letting Israel go. Why do we often settle for minor relief from our problems rather than taking the next step of faith and trust in God?

In what area of your life are you settling for minor relief? Where will you hope in God for deliverance?

EXODUS 9:1-7

THE FIFTH PLAGUE: DEATH OF LIVESTOCK

9 Then the Lord said to Moses, "Go in to Pharaoh and say to him: This is what the Lord, the God of the Hebrews, says: Let my people go, so that they may worship me. ² But if you refuse to let them go and keep holding them, ³ then the Lord's hand will bring a severe plague against your livestock in the field — the horses, donkeys, camels, herds, and flocks. ⁴ But the Lord will make a distinction between the livestock of Israel and the livestock of Egypt, so that nothing of all that the Israelites own will die." ⁵ And the Lord set a time, saying, "Tomorrow the Lord will do this thing in the land." ⁶ The Lord did this the next day. All the Egyptian livestock died, but none among the Israelite livestock died. ⁷ Pharaoh sent messengers who saw that not a single one of the Israelite livestock was dead. But Pharaoh's heart was hard, and he did not let the people go.

DEATH

The Egyptians—and Pharaoh himself—were inconvenienced. But God was going to escalate the plagues. He was about to bring death.

As Pharaoh continued to deny the demands to let God's people go, another plague was promised and delivered. Here, all of Egypt's livestock died—but none belonging to the Hebrews.

God instructed Moses to deliver the warning in a distinct way: "This is what the Lord, the God of the Hebrews says." Again, what Moses said would come to pass.

The lines were drawn.

Pharaoh sent servants to investigate what happened and confirmed that only the Egyptian livestock had died. And yet, even with proof—even with a clear invitation to choose one side or the other—Pharaoh remained stubborn.

The word in Hebrew (the original language of Exodus) describing Pharaoh's hard heart is similar to a word used to describe the burdens he imposed on Israel.

Pharaoh's heart was oppressed and burdened from his own failure to love and trust God. He refused to see what was in front of him. God gave him chances to relent; he chose otherwise. Pharaoh's heart was in the grip of his sin, and God gave him over to his truest desires.

Livestock perished.

REFLECTIONS

Look again at verses 3-4. What happened to Egypt's livestock? What happened to Israel's? What impact must this have had on those who witnessed it?

How did sin and overconfidence blind Pharaoh's heart from responding to God?

This is the fifth of ten plagues against Egypt. Often deliverance is a process. How can we learn to love and trust God in the process?

EXODUS 10:12-20

[12] The LORD then said to Moses, "Stretch out your hand over the land of Egypt, and the locusts will come up over it and eat every plant in the land, everything that the hail left." [13] So Moses stretched out his staff over the land of Egypt, and the LORD sent an east wind over the land all that day and through the night. By morning the east wind had brought in the locusts. [14] The locusts went up over the entire land of Egypt and settled on the whole territory of Egypt. Never before had there been such a large number of locusts, and there never will be again. [15] They covered the surface of the whole land so that the land was black, and they consumed all the plants on the ground and all the fruit on the trees that the hail had left. Nothing green was left on the trees or the plants in the field throughout the land of Egypt.

[16] Pharaoh urgently sent for Moses and Aaron and said, "I have sinned against the LORD your God and against you. [17] Please forgive my sin once more and make an appeal to the LORD your God, so that he will just take this death away from me." [18] Moses left Pharaoh's presence and appealed to the LORD. [19] Then the LORD changed the wind to a strong west wind, and it carried off the locusts and blew them into the Red Sea. Not a single locust was left in all the territory of Egypt. [20] But the LORD hardened Pharaoh's heart, and he did not let the Israelites go.

THE SWARM

The next plague on the Egyptians, a swarm of locusts that blew in from the east all day and night, was so thick that it covered every tree and plant across the land. The locusts devoured everything that the hail—the previous plague—didn't consume.

Shu, one of the gods the Egyptians worshiped, was the god of the wind. The false gods of Egypt could not deliver from the hand of the one true God.

Pharaoh, seeing the hand of the God of the Hebrews, repented. He could no longer maintain the illusion of control. He summoned Moses and Aaron, asking for forgiveness. The brothers prayed, the Lord shifted the gale to a strong west wind, and the locusts were carried off to the Red Sea.

The God of Israel reigns supreme over nature. In the New Testament, we see this with Jesus. The disciples ask of Jesus, *Who is this man, that the wind and the waves obey Him?* When they saw Jesus control a storm, they understood Jesus was God—because only God controls the natural world.

The plagues that befell Egypt were meant to teach the Egyptians, the Israelites, and us that God is in control. There is not one thing in the world over which God does not exercise His authority. Blood, frogs, gnats, flies, livestock, a swarm of devouring locusts, all submit to Him.

How foolish was Pharaoh to not also submit to God? Time and time again, God provided a chance to turn to Him. The plagues were not about the fate of Egypt but the power of God. He is to be revered and worshiped.

Pharaoh realized this, repented, and then quickly relented. His heart was once again hard; God still had more work to do. So we wait in awe to see the wonders from His hands.

Locusts swarmed and devoured.

REFLECTIONS

Each of the ten plagues have been linked to different gods worshiped by the Egyptians. What was God trying to demonstrate to the Egyptians (and the Israelites) through the plagues?

Read back over Pharaoh's plea to Moses. It is longer than others. What does this reveal about Pharaoh's lack of control?

Why should God's ability to bend the natural world to His command help us to trust Him?

CONNECTING THE STORY

In Matthew 8:23-27, Jesus and the disciples were in a boat being tossed by violent wind and waves. The Bible tells us that Jesus "rebuked" the elements (v. 25), and they responded to His command. In Exodus, we find a God who rules over the natural order. In the New Testament, we find that the same God who rules the natural world is present with us in Jesus Christ.

The Plagues
of Egypt

1. BLOOD
   EXODUS 7:14-25

6. BOILS
   EXODUS 9:8-12

2. FROGS
   EXODUS 8:1-15

7. HAIL
   EXODUS 9:13-35

3. GNATS
   EXODUS 8:16-19

8. LOCUSTS
   EXODUS 10:1-20

4. FLIES
   EXODUS 8:20-32

9. DARKNESS
   EXODUS 10:21-29

5. LIVESTOCK
   EXODUS 9:1-7

10. FIRSTBORN
    EXODUS 11 :1-1O; 12:29-32

EXODUS 11:1-10

11 The Lᴏʀᴅ said to Moses, "I will bring one more plague on Pharaoh and on Egypt. After that, he will let you go from here. When he lets you go, he will drive you out of here. ² Now announce to the people that both men and women should ask their neighbors for silver and gold items." ³ The Lᴏʀᴅ gave the people favor with the Egyptians. In addition, Moses himself was very highly regarded in the land of Egypt by Pharaoh's officials and the people.

⁴ So Moses said, "This is what the Lᴏʀᴅ says: About midnight I will go throughout Egypt, ⁵ and every firstborn male in the land of Egypt will die, from the firstborn of Pharaoh who sits on his throne to the firstborn of the servant girl who is at the grindstones, as well as every firstborn of the livestock. ⁶ Then there will be a great cry of anguish through all the land of Egypt such as never was before or ever will be again. ⁷ But against all the Israelites, whether people or animals, not even a dog will snarl, so that you may know that the Lᴏʀᴅ makes a distinction between Egypt and Israel. ⁸ All these officials of yours will come down to me and bow before me, saying: Get out, you and all the people who follow you. After that, I will get out." And he went out from Pharaoh's presence fiercely angry.

⁹ The Lᴏʀᴅ said to Moses, "Pharaoh will not listen to you, so that my wonders may be multiplied in the land of Egypt." ¹⁰ Moses and Aaron did all these wonders before Pharaoh, but the Lᴏʀᴅ hardened Pharaoh's heart, and he would not let the Israelites go out of his land.

FINAL WARNING

Throughout the plagues, we've heard much about the stubbornness of Pharaoh, his willingness to lie, and his callous attitude toward his people.

But what of those people, the Egyptians?

We now learn that God had made the Egyptians look favorably on the Israelites—and on Moses. Moses was highly regarded as a leader, even by Pharaoh's officials. Moses, unlike their own leader, was true to his word and willing to stand for what was right. He hadn't yet seen his people delivered. But he grew in faith and stature every time he made a promise on behalf of God, and God delivered on that promise.

As Moses saw his leadership and influence expand, Pharaoh watched his own diminish. His illusions of power and control were chipped away with every word.

And the last would be the worst word of all. The tenth and final plague would be the death of every firstborn son in Egypt—including Pharaoh's. Loud wailing would spread throughout the land.

Israel, God's own "firstborn," would be spared. It is full circle to the instructions God gave Moses when first returning to Egypt:

> The LORD instructed Moses, "When you go back to Egypt, make sure you
> do before Pharaoh all the wonders that I have put within your power. But
> I will harden his heart, so that he won't let the people go. And you will say
> to Pharaoh: This is what the Lord says: Israel is my firstborn son. I told you:
> Let my son go so that he may worship me, but you refused to let him go.
> Look, I am about to kill your firstborn son!"
> **EXODUS 4:21–23**

God would make Himself known.

And still Pharaoh would not let them go.

REFLECTIONS

Remember back over all the warnings God had given Pharaoh. What does it teach us that these events took place exactly how God declared that they would?

Why do you imagine Pharaoh failed to take God's word seriously even after all he'd experienced?

The plagues reveal the glory of God. Where else has God shown you His glory? Why do we need to take notice of God's glory in our everyday lives?

PAUSE & LISTEN

Spend some time reflecting over the week's reading.

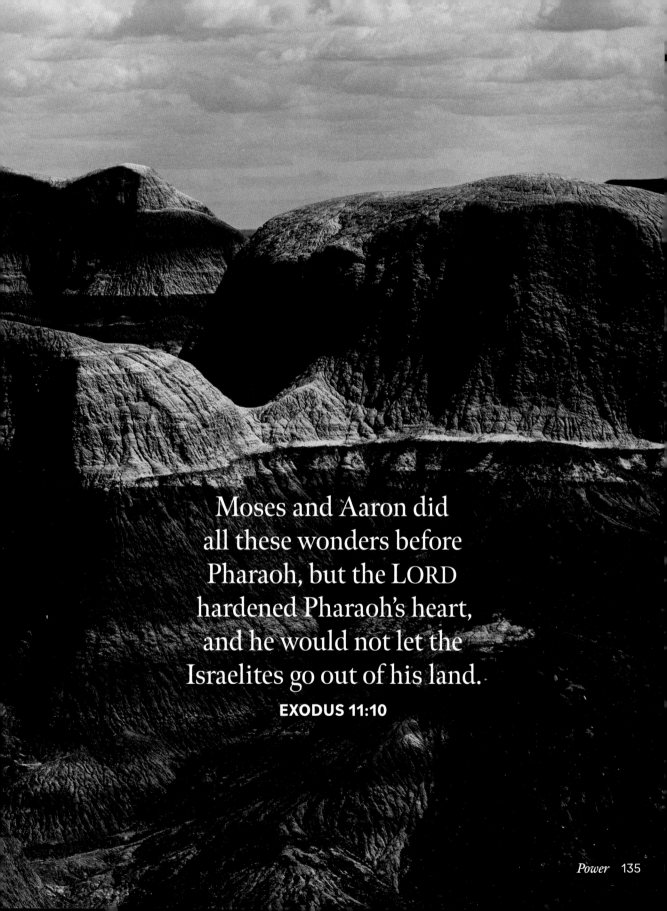

Moses and Aaron did
all these wonders before
Pharaoh, but the LORD
hardened Pharaoh's heart,
and he would not let the
Israelites go out of his land.

EXODUS 11:10

REFLECTION

Use these questions for personal reflection or group discussion on Exodus 7:14–11:10.

What stuck out to you most in this week's reading? What surprised you? Confused you?

What does this week's Scripture teach you about God and His character?

What does this week's Scripture teach you about humanity and our need for grace?

How does this week's Scripture point you to Jesus?

What steps of faith and obedience is God asking you to take through these Scriptures?

PRAY

Pause and reflect on God's power. Confess the things that you love about His character and give Him praise.

WEEK 5

REDEMPTION

Redemption demands sacrifice.

When it comes to the epic stories of the Old Testament, Exodus is as grand as it gets. Everything here is larger than life: the escalating drama, the presence of God, the stakes for disobedience, the rewards for sacrifice.

No wonder, then, that the story is recounted throughout the Bible as a touchpoint of redemption and promises kept, a reminder that this is the Lord who brought His people up out of Egypt.

Within these pages, the struggle for freedom reached its height with the carefully orchestrated "passing over" of the houses of Israel, sparing the firstborn sons the fate of their Egyptian contemporaries. These Israelites sacrificed a spotless lamb and marked their doorposts with its blood—paving the way for Jesus to become the "Passover Lamb" for humanity, His perfect blood shed for the freedom of all.

> But because the Lord loved you and kept the oath he swore to your ancestors, he brought you out with a strong hand and redeemed you from the place of slavery, from the power of Pharaoh king of Egypt. Know that the Lord your God is God, the faithful God who keeps his gracious covenant loyalty for a thousand generations with those who love him and keep his commands.
> **DEUTERONOMY 7:8-9**

The events we read about this week provide the framework for how redemption is understood throughout the entire Bible. Notice the themes of sacrifice, atonement, grace, and substitution. The Passover will be reflected upon and referred to throughout the rest of the Bible. To unlock the riches of the Bible, we need to see the riches in this account.

EXODUS 12:1-13

INSTRUCTIONS FOR THE PASSOVER

12 The Lord said to Moses and Aaron in the land of Egypt, ² "This month is to be the beginning of months for you; it is the first month of your year. ³ Tell the whole community of Israel that on the tenth day of this month they must each select an animal of the flock according to their fathers' families, one animal per family. ⁴ If the household is too small for a whole animal, that person and the neighbor nearest his house are to select one based on the combined number of people; you should apportion the animal according to what each will eat. ⁵ You must have an unblemished animal, a year-old male; you may take it from either the sheep or the goats. ⁶ You are to keep it until the fourteenth day of this month; then the whole assembly of the community of Israel will slaughter the animals at twilight. ⁷ They must take some of the blood and put it on the two doorposts and the lintel of the houses where they eat them. ⁸ They are to eat the meat that night; they should eat it, roasted over the fire along with unleavened bread and bitter herbs. ⁹ Do not eat any of it raw or cooked in boiling water, but only roasted over fire — its head as well as its legs and inner organs. ¹⁰ You must not leave any of it until morning; any part of it left until morning you must burn. ¹¹ Here is how you must eat it: You must be dressed for travel, your sandals on your feet, and your staff in your hand. You are to eat it in a hurry; it is the Lord's Passover.

¹² "I will pass through the land of Egypt on that night and strike every firstborn male in the land of Egypt, both people and animals. I am the Lord; I will execute judgments against all the gods of Egypt. ¹³ The blood on the houses where you are staying will be a distinguishing mark for you; when I see the blood, I will pass over you. No plague will be among you to destroy you when I strike the land of Egypt."

<table>
<tr><td>DAY
29</td><td># FAITH</td></tr>
</table>

FAITH

Judgment was about to be on the doorstep.

With many of the previous plagues, the Israelites had been spared simply because they had been set apart by God.

But this time—the tenth and final plague—the Israelites were invited to exercise faith in God. They had to follow God's instructions to be spared the fate of the Egyptians. They must find an unblemished lamb and take it into their homes to observe it for defects. Once the lamb had been observed, they would then sacrifice it, spread it's blood on the door frame of their home, and prepare a meal with the meat.

This sacrifice would protect them from certain death. The instructions were as much about the preparation of the Israelites as they were the preparation of the lamb. They were told how to make a meal—and how to eat it the night that the death of the firstborn sons would occur. They were to eat fully dressed—even wearing their sandals. They were to eat with urgency, and to have their walking sticks in hand. They were to be ready.

This judgment would not be passive. For the Israelites, it would require faith and sacrifice. It would mean setting aside fear and uncertainty, and replacing it with trust in the God who had so far spared them from the previous plagues.

As God invited these Israelites to be personally invested, He invites us to do the same.

By God's grace, we place our faith in a substitute that God has provided.

We place our faith in a substitute
that God has provided.

REFLECTIONS

List all the steps you read in this passage. What do you think the people were supposed to learn following these steps?

When has faith been a process for you? What did you learn from following the process?

What is a step of faith or belief you need to take this week in order to deepen your love and trust for God?

INSIGHT

In verse 11, the event is described as "the LORD's Passover." This statement highlights that the focus of these events is God and the beneficiaries are the Hebrews. Like the rest of the Bible, Exodus is primarily a story about God.

EXODUS 12:14-20

[14] "This day is to be a memorial for you, and you must celebrate it as a festival to the Lord. You are to celebrate it throughout your generations as a permanent statute. [15] You must eat unleavened bread for seven days. On the first day you must remove yeast from your houses. Whoever eats what is leavened from the first day through the seventh day must be cut off from Israel. [16] You are to hold a sacred assembly on the first day and another sacred assembly on the seventh day. No work may be done on those days except for preparing what people need to eat — you may do only that.

[17] "You are to observe the Festival of Unleavened Bread because on this very day I brought your military divisions out of the land of Egypt. You must observe this day throughout your generations as a permanent statute. [18] You are to eat unleavened bread in the first month, from the evening of the fourteenth day of the month until the evening of the twenty-first day. [19] Yeast must not be found in your houses for seven days. If anyone eats something leavened, that person, whether a resident alien or native of the land, must be cut off from the community of Israel. [20] Do not eat anything leavened; eat unleavened bread in all your homes."

TIME

At the end of the Bible, we are told that God's people will overcome evil by the blood of the Lamb and by the word of their testimony (Revelation 12:11). What happens at the end of the story is mirrored in what we find here in Exodus.

God's people have always been shaped by the blood of the lamb and the word of their testimony. Yesterday touched on the lamb, but we cannot miss the importance of testimony. We have to see how this story shaped the story of God's people.

The tenth plague would change the way Israelites marked time. What God was about to do among them was so significant that it would completely reorient their lives. It would transform them from enslaved people to free people.

The deliverance they were to experience would be so significant that they needed to reflect on it year after year. It was to be memorialized, rehearsed, and celebrated from that time forward. The testimony of God's deliverance was to be shared across time and place.

The commemoration also includes reflection and retelling of how the Israelites were spared. God doesn't need to be reminded of His powerful works.

We do.

This story prepared God's people for when Jesus, the true Passover lamb, celebrated Passover with His disciples. He taught his followers to take communion to memorialize and celebrate His sacrifice—once again commemorating salvation through the shedding of innocent blood.

> And he took bread, gave thanks, broke it, gave it to them, and said, "This is my body, which is given for you. Do this in remembrance of me." In the same way he also took the cup after supper and said, "This cup is the new covenant in my blood, which is poured out for you."
> **LUKE 22:19-20**

The table was set. The meal was prepared. And the blood would soon be shed.

God's deliverance was to be shared
across time and place.

REFLECTIONS

Why did God ask His people to celebrate Passover in perpetuity?

How did Jesus repurpose the Passover story when He shared what we now know as Communion or the Lord's Supper with His disciples?

How does sharing a story about what God has done help us to remember and be grateful for His work in our lives?

INSIGHT

After the first Passover, Jews were called to remember and celebrate Passover every year. Commandments and regulations concerning how to celebrate Passover are given in the next three books, Leviticus, Numbers, and Deuteronomy. Jesus celebrated Passover with His disciples in each gospel account. Prior to Jesus's death and resurrection, Passover was the primary way followers of God remembered His redemption.

EXODUS 12:21-28

²¹ Then Moses summoned all the elders of Israel and said to them, "Go, select an animal from the flock according to your families, and slaughter the Passover animal. ²² Take a cluster of hyssop, dip it in the blood that is in the basin, and brush the lintel and the two doorposts with some of the blood in the basin. None of you may go out the door of his house until morning. ²³ When the Lord passes through to strike Egypt and sees the blood on the lintel and the two doorposts, he will pass over the door and not let the destroyer enter your houses to strike you.

²⁴ "Keep this command permanently as a statute for you and your descendants. ²⁵ When you enter the land that the Lord will give you as he promised, you are to observe this ceremony. ²⁶ When your children ask you, 'What does this ceremony mean to you?' ²⁷ you are to reply, 'It is the Passover sacrifice to the Lord, for he passed over the houses of the Israelites in Egypt when he struck the Egyptians, and he spared our homes.'" So the people knelt low and worshiped. ²⁸ Then the Israelites went and did this; they did just as the Lord had commanded Moses and Aaron.

RESPONSE

Moses relayed to leaders of the Israelites all that God had shared about this final plague. He spoke of the slaughter of the lamb, the draining of its blood, the application to the door frame, and the way God would pass through the land to strike down the Egyptians.

He told them too about this being a permanent law—and that the ceremony would still be observed "when" they entered the land that God had promised to give them. There was no "if" in his words, no room for doubt.

The Israelites responded by bowing down and worshiping God. Not pleading for mercy or arguing their case. They believed what they had been told. They didn't hold off until they saw it come to pass. They didn't wait until morning, when they could confirm that God was faithful.

They had seen display after display of God's miraculous power and authority, with one plague following another. They had watched God set them apart from the Egyptians, sparing them from the destruction of their livestock as well as from boils, hail, locusts, and days of darkness.

And they responded. The Israelites were not being passed over because they were better than the Egyptians, but because God graciously provided the means for their redemption. God's faithfulness shaped their response.

Worshiping God—not just for what He has done or will do, but simply for who He is—is an act of true faith. Worship is always a response to who God is.

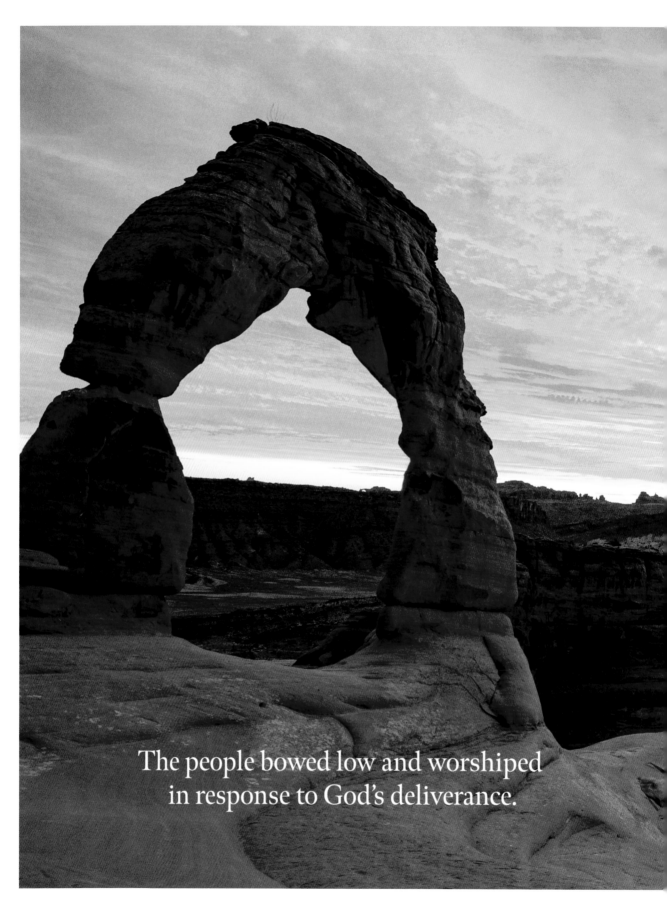

The people bowed low and worshiped
in response to God's deliverance.

REFLECTIONS

What had the people of Israel seen God do in order to bring about their deliverance?

Respond to the phrase: "Faith in God always requires a response."

Why is worship something that should characterize our lives and not just something that we do on Sundays? How will you worship God during the next week?

EXODUS 12:29-32

THE EXODUS

²⁹ Now at midnight the Lᴏʀᴅ struck every firstborn male in the land of Egypt, from the firstborn of Pharaoh who sat on his throne to the firstborn of the prisoner who was in the dungeon, and every firstborn of the livestock. ³⁰ During the night Pharaoh got up, he along with all his officials and all the Egyptians, and there was a loud wailing throughout Egypt because there wasn't a house without someone dead. ³¹ He summoned Moses and Aaron during the night and said, "Get out immediately from among my people, both you and the Israelites, and go, worship the Lᴏʀᴅ as you have said. ³² Take even your flocks and your herds as you asked and leave, and also bless me."

<table>
<tr><td>DAY</td></tr>
<tr><td>32</td></tr>
</table>

LOSS

At the stroke of midnight, God did what He had promised. All of the firstborn sons in Egypt—from Pharaoh to the prisoners in the dungeon—were slain.

There was not a single house in Egypt, we're told, where someone had not died.

Imagine the anguished cries. The grief. It was incalculable.

The sobering fact of redemption is that for one life to flourish, another must be given in its place. A price must be paid. Israel paid the price by taking the life of an innocent lamb and sheltering under it's blood for protection. Pharaoh and the Egyptians did not trust God's word. Because of this God's signs and wonders were multiplied across the land of Egypt. Pharaoh was unable to protect his people. The loss was unbearable.

That very night, Pharaoh sent for Moses and Aaron, and ordered them to leave. He told them to take the Israelites with them and all their flocks and herds.

The Israelites had accepted the substitute, the exchange that God offered through the blood of the lamb.

It's up to us to do the same. Jesus offers us all the opportunity to shelter under His blood for protection and deliverance. Our redemption came at the cost of God's only Son. The narrative threads that begin in Exodus are finished in Jesus.

However, the redemption Jesus offers is a permanent, life-shaping redemption. All who place themselves under the protection of His blood will never again be separated from God.

At the stroke of midnight,
God did what He promised.

REFLECTIONS

The Bible only tells us about Pharaoh's response to the loss, but what do you imagine the response must have been like throughout Egypt?

What does the cost of redemption teach us about the value of redemption?

What did your redemption cost Jesus, and how does that shape how you respond to Jesus?

Passover

The Passover creates a template for sacrifices to God where God accepts the blood of a sacrifice in the place or burden of another. This is a reoccurring theme throughout the rest of the Scriptures, including numerous places where Jesus is referred to as a lamb.

Isaiah predicted Jesus's sacrifice.

ISAIAH 53:7.
He was oppressed and afflicted,
yet he did not open his mouth.
Like a lamb led to the slaughter
and like a sheep silent before her shearers,
he did not open his mouth.

John the Baptist identified Jesus as a lamb.

JOHN 1:29. The next day John saw Jesus coming toward him and said, "Look, the Lamb of God, who takes away the sin of the world!"

Paul argued that Christ made us clean.

1 CORINTHIANS 5:7. Clean out the old leaven so that you may be a new unleavened batch, as indeed you are. For Christ our Passover lamb has been sacrificed.

Peter wrote that Jesus was a better sacrifice.

1 PETER 1:18-19. For you know that you were redeemed from your empty way of life inherited from your ancestors, not with perishable things like silver or gold, but with the precious blood of Christ, like that of an unblemished and spotless lamb.

John repeatedly pointed to Jesus as the lamb.

REVELATION. There are twenty-nine individual references to Jesus being the Lamb of God throughout the book.

EXODUS 12:33-42

[33] Now the Egyptians pressured the people in order to send them quickly out of the country, for they said, "We're all going to die!" [34] So the people took their dough before it was leavened, with their kneading bowls wrapped up in their clothes on their shoulders.

[35] The Israelites acted on Moses's word and asked the Egyptians for silver and gold items and for clothing. [36] And the Lord gave the people such favor with the Egyptians that they gave them what they requested. In this way they plundered the Egyptians.

[37] The Israelites traveled from Rameses to Succoth, about six hundred thousand able-bodied men on foot, besides their families. [38] A mixed crowd also went up with them, along with a huge number of livestock, both flocks and herds. [39] The people baked the dough they had brought out of Egypt into unleavened loaves, since it had no yeast; for when they were driven out of Egypt, they could not delay and had not prepared provisions for themselves.

[40] The time that the Israelites lived in Egypt was 430 years. [41] At the end of 430 years, on that same day, all the Lord's military divisions went out from the land of Egypt. [42] It was a night of vigil in honor of the Lord, because he would bring them out of the land of Egypt. This same night is in honor of the Lord, a night vigil for all the Israelites throughout their generations.

REDEMPTION REALIZED

Four hundred and thirty years. That's how long Israel lived in Egypt. How many times in those centuries as enslaved people had the Israelites wondered, *Did God hear? Did He care?*

For hundreds of years, the Israelites grew the wealth and prosperity of Egypt. And in an instant, God had released them with the wealth of Egypt in tow. What had been taken was being returned. The time had finally come. The Israelites had been released from Pharaoh's grip.

Some eighty years before, when Moses was an infant, Pharaoh had called for the life of all Hebrew boys. And yet here some 600,000 Hebrew men began their trek out of Egypt as free men.

God is always faithful to His word. His timing may not align with our timing, but we can never take this as evidence that God does not hear or does not care. As we read in Exodus 2, God saw, God heard, and God knew.

Through years of hard labor, slavery, and oppression, God saw. He prepared a deliverer, and He delivered.

It was time for new life to begin. One as a free people. One as a nation built by God and set apart in a land that He provided. The wealth taken from Egypt would become the raw materials for the tent of meeting God would have His people create to meet with Him. God was always present. Always listening. Always working.

God delivered.

REFLECTIONS

It took the Israelites 430 years to be freed from Egypt. What does that tell us about God's timetable?

When has God been faithful to you even though you had to wait?

What are you waiting on right now? What evidence of God's faithfulness can you hold on to as you wait?

DAY
34

PAUSE & LISTEN
Spend some time reflecting over the week's reading.

"When your children ask you,
'What does this ceremony mean to you?'
you are to reply, 'It is the Passover sacrifice
to the LORD, for he passed over the houses
of the Israelites in Egypt when he struck
the Egyptians, and he spared our homes.'"
So the people knelt low and worshiped.

EXODUS 12:26-27

REFLECTION

Use these questions for personal reflection or group discussion on Exodus 12.

What stuck out to you most in this week's reading? What surprised you? Confused you?

What does this week's Scripture teach you about God and His character?

What does this week's Scripture teach you about humanity and our need for grace?

How does this week's Scripture point you to Jesus?

What steps of faith and obedience is God asking you to take through these Scriptures?

PRAY

Pause for a moment and call to mind a few things God has done for you. Spend a few more moments thanking God for His work in your life.

WEEK 6

WORSHIP

Worship is our response to who
God is and what He has done.

Worship takes on many forms.

We might think of it as just songs we sing about—or to—God. But worship can also be seen in our sacrifices, our obedience, and even our remembrance and retelling of the great things God has done. It is everything and anything we do to honor God and give Him praise.

When Moses went before Pharaoh to demand the release of the Israelites, he gave a singular reason again and again: so that they might worship God. This was not Moses's idea; it was God's. But He did not dictate worship in the way of an evil, arrogant ruler.

Rather, God invites worship that we might better understand who He is—and who we are in relationship to Him.

As an Egyptian leader, Pharaoh would have been well acquainted with the idea of worship; as a culture, the Egyptians worshiped many gods. In addition, Pharaohs were considered like gods on earth.

The one true God, however, would make Himself known.

As the Israelites escaped Egypt, one more miraculous show of power was right around the corner. And God had planned this, the Word tells us, so that even the Egyptians would know that He is Lord.

He is worthy to be praised.

EXODUS 13:1-10

13 The Lord spoke to Moses: ² "Consecrate every firstborn male to me, the firstborn from every womb among the Israelites, both man and domestic animal; it is mine."

³ Then Moses said to the people, "Remember this day when you came out of Egypt, out of the place of slavery, for the Lord brought you out of here by the strength of his hand. Nothing leavened may be eaten. ⁴ Today, in the month of Abib, you are going out. ⁵ When the Lord brings you into the land of the Canaanites, Hethites, Amorites, Hivites, and Jebusites, which he swore to your ancestors that he would give you, a land flowing with milk and honey, you must carry out this ceremony in this month. ⁶ For seven days you must eat unleavened bread, and on the seventh day there is to be a festival to the Lord. ⁷ Unleavened bread is to be eaten for those seven days. Nothing leavened may be found among you, and no yeast may be found among you in all your territory. ⁸ On that day explain to your son, 'This is because of what the Lord did for me when I came out of Egypt.' ⁹ Let it serve as a sign for you on your hand and as a reminder on your forehead, so that the Lord's instruction may be in your mouth; for the Lord brought you out of Egypt with a strong hand. ¹⁰ Keep this statute at its appointed time from year to year."

SIGNPOST

God wasted no time in setting up structures and patterns for the Israelites as they set out for the Promised Land.

He began by telling Moses to dedicate every firstborn among the Israelites to Him. The firstborn of the Egyptians were struck down, that the firstborn sons of the Israelites might be redeemed—and that they might be regularly reminded of God's deliverance.

Those firstborn sons, after all, may well be the leaders of tomorrow, the ones to carry on tradition and understanding, to share the story of God's redemption. The firstborn—whether human or animal—symbolized all that was to follow.

God took the time to lay out specific instructions for the ways the Israelites would be set apart, not just today but for all time. Remembering what God had done—and taking the time to commemorate it year after year—would be like a sign on the hands of the Israelites.

The Israelites' relationship with God would set them apart. But God also told the Israelites that the observance was to be "a reminder on your forehead, so that the LORD's instruction may be in your mouth."

It was not enough for the Israelites—or for us—to show outward signs of obedience. We're also called to inner transformation, to meditate on His deeds and faithfulness, and to let His teachings come from our mouths.

Year after year, He is faithful; He calls us to be the same. Worship is more about what occurs in our hearts than what is obvious in our lives. Both are necessary, but the inner change happens first.

God is faithful.

REFLECTIONS

List the ways God gave the Israelites to commemorate what happened to them.

What does it mean to meditate on God's deeds?

In what ways do you personally remember and celebrate what God has done in your life?

EXODUS 13:14-16

[14] "In the future, when your son asks you, 'What does this mean?' say to him, 'By the strength of his hand the Lord brought us out of Egypt, out of the place of slavery. [15] When Pharaoh stubbornly refused to let us go, the Lord killed every firstborn male in the land of Egypt, both the firstborn of humans and the first-born of livestock. That is why I sacrifice to the Lord all the firstborn of the womb that are males, but I redeem all the firstborn of my sons.' [16] So let it be a sign on your hand and a symbol on your forehead, for the Lord brought us out of Egypt by the strength of his hand."

SIGN AND SYMBOL

Today's reading may seem redundant. We've already read about these events in the Bible and in the pages of this study. But the repetition is important. What we read in these verses becomes a pattern throughout the rest of Scripture. Israel is to take what happened, internalize it, then share it over and over for all time.

Throughout the rest of the Old Testament, we see God referring to Himself as "the Lord your God who brought you out of slavery." For a Hebrew, this was the seminal moment in their history. Everything before led up to it and everything after flowed from it. This happened through repetition and storytelling. We're reading about it again along with the Israelites. This wouldn't be the first or last time they heard these truths.

They were to hear them repeatedly so that they could remember them, internalize them, and recite them. The work of God in their lives should have been as close to them as their own thoughts. It was a sign and a symbol to be remembered throughout generations.

A similar pattern emerges in the New Testament. The resurrection is a onetime event, but everything else in the Christian life flows from it. Israel was different because they were a free and redeemed people. They were no longer enslaved. Sharing that story cultivated gratitude toward God for His deliverance.

Reflecting on the gospel—the story of the life, death, resurrection, rule, reign, and return of Jesus—accomplishes the same purpose for the Christian. Exodus puts forth a pattern of repetition and remembrance that continues in the New Testament church.

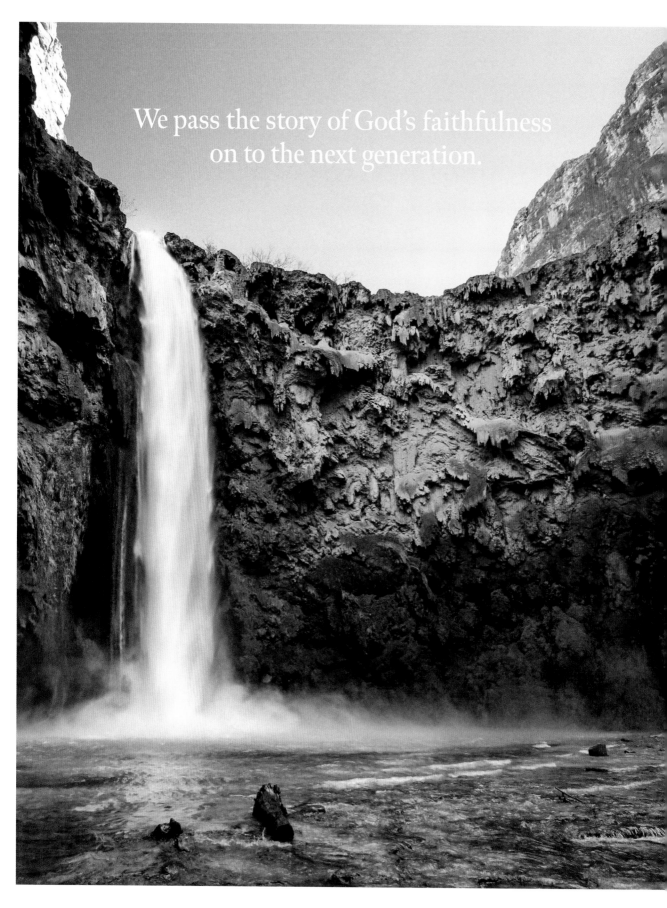

We pass the story of God's faithfulness
on to the next generation.

REFLECTIONS

We've seen several instances of repetition in Exodus. Why is reading and rereading the same ideas multiple times helpful?

How does repetition and remembrance help us internalize important truths?

What truths about God do you need to repeat and remember?

EXODUS 14:5-14

THE EGYPTIAN PURSUIT

[5] When the king of Egypt was told that the people had fled, Pharaoh and his officials changed their minds about the people and said, "What have we done? We have released Israel from serving us." [6] So he got his chariot ready and took his troops with him; [7] he took six hundred of the best chariots and all the rest of the chariots of Egypt, with officers in each one. [8] The LORD hardened the heart of Pharaoh king of Egypt, and he pursued the Israelites, who were going out defiantly. [9] The Egyptians — all Pharaoh's horses and chariots, his horsemen, and his army — chased after them and caught up with them as they camped by the sea beside Pi-hahiroth, in front of Baal-zephon.

[10] As Pharaoh approached, the Israelites looked up and there were the Egyptians coming after them! The Israelites were terrified and cried out to the LORD for help. [11] They said to Moses, "Is it because there are no graves in Egypt that you have taken us away to die in the wilderness? What have you done to us by bringing us out of Egypt? [12] Isn't this what we told you in Egypt: Leave us alone so that we may serve the Egyptians? It would have been better for us to serve the Egyptians than to die in the wilderness."

[13] But Moses said to the people, "Don't be afraid. Stand firm and see the LORD's salvation that he will accomplish for you today; for the Egyptians you see today, you will never see again. [14] The LORD will fight for you, and you must be quiet."

STAND FIRM

Life with God is often not a straight path. It's filled with twists and turns, hills and valleys. But what seem like obstacles to us are not obstacles to God.

No sooner had the Israelites been released from Egypt that Pharaoh relented once again. At this point, this should read like a familiar and repeating pattern to you. Pharaoh promised release then changed his mind. It's happened throughout the book. It was happening again. Except this time, Pharaoh had assembled the might of Egypt to enslave the Israelites again.

Yet when he pursued, the Israelites seemed to have forgotten about the deliverance they had already experienced. They didn't see the pattern. The Hebrews were afraid and began to grumble to their leader Moses. They began formulating plans to return to Egypt.

This is what we all do when confronted with hardship. We foolishly believe it would be better to turn back to the things that rob us from life. We're so used to the valley we have trouble climbing out.

Moses however recognized what was happening and responded with surprising faith, given what we've seen from Moses in the past. He encouraged the Israelites that this would be the last time the Egyptians terrorized them. Moses recognized that God cared more about their struggles and their predicament than they did. He will work. All that is needed is our silent cooperation.

Sometimes trust in God calls us to stop and remember what He's done while we wait for Him to do it again. The dangers are real, but so is God.

The Lord fights for us. We just have to be still.

REFLECTIONS

After all the Israelites had seen, why did they continue to fear Pharaoh?

How do we forget the pattern of God's work like the Israelites did many years ago?

Where are you actively working to bring about a preferred outcome when it would be better for you to simply be still?

EXODUS 14:15-31

ESCAPE THROUGH THE RED SEA

[15] The Lord said to Moses, "Why are you crying out to me? Tell the Israelites to break camp. [16] As for you, lift up your staff, stretch out your hand over the sea, and divide it so that the Israelites can go through the sea on dry ground. [17] As for me, I am going to harden the hearts of the Egyptians so that they will go in after them, and I will receive glory by means of Pharaoh, all his army, and his chariots and horsemen. [18] The Egyptians will know that I am the Lord when I receive glory through Pharaoh, his chariots, and his horsemen."

[19] Then the angel of God, who was going in front of the Israelite forces, moved and went behind them. The pillar of cloud moved from in front of them and stood behind them. [20] It came between the Egyptian and Israelite forces. There was cloud and darkness, it lit up the night, and neither group came near the other all night long.

[21] Then Moses stretched out his hand over the sea. The Lord drove the sea back with a powerful east wind all that night and turned the sea into dry land. So the waters were divided, [22] and the Israelites went through the sea on dry ground, with the waters like a wall to them on their right and their left.

[23] The Egyptians set out in pursuit — all Pharaoh's horses, his chariots, and his horsemen — and went into the sea after them. [24] During the morning watch, the Lord looked down at the Egyptian forces from the pillar of fire and cloud, and threw the Egyptian forces into confusion. [25] He caused their chariot wheels to swerve and made them drive with difficulty. "Let's get away from Israel," the Egyptians said, "because the Lord is fighting for them against Egypt!"

[26] Then the Lord said to Moses, "Stretch out your hand over the sea so that the water may come back on the Egyptians, on their chariots and horsemen." [27] So Moses stretched out his hand over the sea, and at daybreak the sea returned to its normal depth. While the Egyptians were trying to escape from it, the Lord threw them into the sea. [28] The water came back and covered the chariots and horsemen, plus the entire army of Pharaoh that had gone after them into the sea. Not even one of them survived.

[29] But the Israelites had walked through the sea on dry ground, with the waters like a wall to them on their right and their left. [30] That day the Lord saved Israel from the power of the Egyptians, and Israel saw the Egyptians dead on the seashore. [31] When Israel saw the great power that the Lord used against the Egyptians, the people feared the Lord and believed in him and in his servant Moses.

A DEFINITIVE SOLUTION

Stand firm? Absolutely. Stand still? Not a chance.

The Israelites were hemmed in. The Egyptians were geared up for a fight. There appeared to be nowhere to escape. But that's when God does His best work.

He told Moses it was time for the people to move. It was also time for him to pick up his staff, raise his hand over the Red Sea, and divide the waters. The pillar of cloud that had been leading the way moved between the Israelites and Egyptians, and as day turns to night, the pillar turned to fire.

A powerful wind separated the waves, and the Israelites began to walk through on dry ground. The Egyptians, meanwhile, were thrown into confusion. When the Israelites reached the other side, Moses raised his hand once more and the waters closed in on the Egyptians, killing every last one.

The solution was definitive. The deliverance was complete. And this passing through to the other side—to new life—had happened in an undeniably supernatural way. All would know that He was God, the One who had brought them up out of Egypt. None of this would've happened if the Israelites left Egypt without hardship. God wanted them to understand that their deliverance was complete and settled. That which enslaved them is no long a danger to them.

Here, too, we see a foreshadowing of another rebirth: that new life promised us by Jesus, the one possible only through struggle, perseverance, faith—and supernatural power. On the other side of Jesus's deliverance, what used to enslave us is no longer a danger to us. We are free.

That day the Lord
saved Israel.

REFLECTIONS

What do you find most incredible about this account? Why is it good to be awed by the Bible?

What does this passage teach us about God's power and desire to deliver?

What do you need to trust God to deliver you from? Is there an area of turmoil or internal strife where you could use the Lord's help?

Out of Slavery

After Israel had been freed from slavery, God gave them the Ten Commandments. The account begins this way: "Then God spoke all these words: I am the LORD your God, who brought you out of the land of Egypt, out of the place of slavery" (Exodus 20:1-2). God refers to Himself this way hundreds of times. Being redeemed out of slavery and into freedom was the primary way God wanted His people to understand their redemption.

It described God's character.

LEVITICUS 11:45. For I am the Lord, who brought you up from the land of Egypt to be your God, so you must be holy because I am holy.

It was used to mark time.

NUMBERS 1:1. The Lord spoke to Moses in the tent of meeting in the Wilderness of Sinai, on the first day of the second month of the second year after Israel's departure from the land of Egypt.

It reminded Israel of their identity.

DEUTERONOMY 5:6. I am the Lord your God, who brought you out of the land of Egypt, out of the place of slavery.

Other nations heard about what God had done.

JOSHUA 9:9. [The Hivites] replied to [Joshua], "Your servants have come from a faraway land because of the reputation of the Lord your God. For we have heard of his fame, and all that he did in Egypt."

Even hundreds of years later it was used to mark time.

1 KINGS 6:1. Solomon began to build the temple for the Lord in the four hundred eightieth year after the Israelites came out of the land of Egypt, in the fourth year of his reign over Israel, in the month of Ziv, which is the second month.

It was used in songs of praise.

PSALM 81:10. I am the Lord your God, who brought you up from the land of Egypt. Open your mouth wide, and I will fill it.

The prophets used it to signify God's future faithfulness.

HOSEA 2:15. There I will give her vineyards back to her and make the Valley of Achor into a gateway of hope. There she will respond as she did in the days of her youth, as in the day she came out of the land of Egypt.

It was also reflected back on in the New Testament.

IN HEBREWS 8:7-13, God showed the redemption Jesus offers is even better than the redemption from Egypt.

ISRAEL'S SONG

15 Then Moses and the Israelites sang this song to the LORD. They said:

I will sing to the LORD,
for he is highly exalted;
he has thrown the horse
and its rider into the sea.
2 The LORD is my strength and my song;
he has become my salvation.
This is my God, and I will praise him,
my father's God, and I will exalt him.
3 The LORD is a warrior;
the LORD is his name.

4 He threw Pharaoh's chariots
and his army into the sea;
the elite of his officers
were drowned in the Red Sea.
5 The floods covered them;
they sank to the depths like a stone.
6 LORD, your right hand is glorious in power.
LORD, your right hand shattered the enemy.
7 You overthrew your adversaries
by your great majesty.
You unleashed your burning wrath;
it consumed them like stubble.
8 The water heaped up at the blast from your nostrils;
the currents stood firm like a dam.
The watery depths congealed in the heart
of the sea.
9 The enemy said:
"I will pursue, I will overtake,
I will divide the spoil.
My desire will be gratified at their expense.
I will draw my sword;
my hand will destroy them."
10 But you blew with your breath,
and the sea covered them.
They sank like lead
in the mighty waters.

11 LORD, who is like you among the gods?
Who is like you, glorious in holiness,
revered with praises, performing wonders?
12 You stretched out your right hand,
v the earth swallowed them.
13 With your faithful love,
you will lead the people
you have redeemed;
you will guide them to your holy dwelling
with your strength.

14 When the peoples hear, they will shudder;
anguish will seize the inhabitants of Philistia.
15 Then the chiefs of Edom will be terrified;
trembling will seize the leaders of Moab;
all the inhabitants of Canaan will panic;
16 terror and dread will fall on them.
They will be as still as a stone
because of your powerful arm
until your people pass by, LORD,
until the people whom you purchased pass by.

17 You will bring them in and plant them
on the mountain of your possession;
LORD, you have prepared the place
for your dwelling;
Lord, your hands have established the sanctuary.
18 The LORD will reign forever and ever!

19 When Pharaoh's horses with his chariots and horsemen went into the sea, the LORD brought the water of the sea back over them. But the Israelites walked through the sea on dry ground. 20 Then the prophetess Miriam, Aaron's sister, took a tambourine in her hand, and all the women came out following her with tambourines and dancing. 21 Miriam sang to them:

Sing to the LORD,
for he is highly exalted;
he has thrown the horse
and its rider into the sea.

PAST VICTORY, PRESENT FAITH

DAY 40

The man who felt insecure about speaking was now bursting forth in song.

How could Moses help but worship? The Word shares his song of deliverance, telling the tale of horse and rider being hurled into the sea, of surging waters that stood straight up like a wall, of God leading the redeemed with unfailing love.

In truth, the challenges of the Israelites were far from over. There would be endless days ahead in that wilderness. There would be faithlessness and doubt. But in that moment, God's victory was tangible—and worth remembering time and time again.

Days will come when we too feel faithless, full of doubt, and backed into a corner.

And yet, the more we remind ourselves of God's past victories, the easier those stories are to recall—and the faster our faith will grow.

God's plan for Moses was established long before he arrived on earth. It is the same for Jesus.

And it is the same for us.

We may not believe that we have miraculous stories of our own to tell, or at least not yet. But we, just like the Israelites, can remember, recount, and be inspired by the faith stories of others.

And the stories of Exodus grow faith—and confirm the promises and presence of God—with every telling. They invite us into the deeper story of God's great love and redemption.

The Lord will reign forever and ever.

REFLECTIONS

List several things for which Moses praised God in this passage.

What about God makes you want to worship Him?

What has this study taught you about God's ultimate plans for redeeming His people?

PAUSE & LISTEN

Spend some time reflecting over the week's reading.

The LORD will reign
forever and ever!

EXODUS 15:18

REFLECTION

Use these questions for personal reflection or group discussion on Exodus 13–15.

What stuck out to you most in this week's reading? What surprised you? Confused you?

What does this week's Scripture teach you about God and His character?

What does this week's Scripture teach you about humanity and our need for grace?

How does this week's Scripture point you to Jesus?

What steps of faith and obedience is God asking you to take through these Scriptures?

PRAY

End your time in Exodus worshiping God. Praise God for accomplishing our redemption and bringing us out of slavery to sin and death.

PHOTOGRAPHY CREDITS

FOUNDATIONS
BIBLE READING PLAN FOR GROUPS
FOUNDATIONS
OLD TESTAMENT
A 260-DAY BIBLE READING PLAN FOR BUSY BELIEVERS
ROBBY & KANDI GALLATY
REPLICATE

Manageable one-year plans for Bible reading

Foundations gives you a one-year Bible reading plan that requires just five days of study per week to fit your busy schedule. It includes daily devotional material. And through the HEAR journaling method, you'll learn how to Highlight, Explain, Apply, and Respond to passages, allowing for practical application.

Foundations
Study key passages of the Bible in one year,
while still having the flexibility of reading five days per week.

005769893 **$14.99**

Foundations: New Testament
Read and reflect on the New Testament in one year
with this reading and devotional guide.

005810327 **$14.99**

Foundations: Old Testament
Read through the story of the Old Testament in one year
using this manageable five-day-per-week plan.

005831469 **$14.99**

lifeway.com/foundations
Learn more online or call 800.458.2772.

EXPERIENCING GOD

SOME STUDIES HELP YOU KNOW THE BIBLE.
THIS ONE HELPS YOU KNOW THE AUTHOR.

For more than three decades, God has used the truths of *Experiencing God* to awaken believers to a radically God-centered way of life. As a result, millions have come to know God intimately, to recognize His voice, and to understand His will for their lives. This new edition is revised, updated, and ready to lead you again—or for the very first time—into a deeper relationship with God.

THE NEXT STORY TO TELL

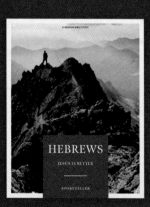

The book of Hebrews makes a simple request—consider Jesus. Throughout the letter, the author systematically works through key themes and characters in the Bible and points out how Jesus is better than all of them. You may be wondering about the same things yourself. This Bible study (the next in the Storyteller series) will help you see that Jesus is more than worthy of your consideration.

Learn more online or call 800.458.2772.
lifeway.com/storyteller

Your deliverance is near.

The story of Exodus is rich with present-day promise and relevance—especially for anyone who is feeling stuck, standing in faith, or longing to see a promise kept.

An insecure and paranoid king ruled over Egypt, enslaved the Israelites, and imposed brutal work conditions upon them. But every day God's people languished, He had a plan for delivering them. He was in the details, preparing the way for their redemption. He worked through men and mighty miracles to free the Israelites from the Egyptians. He worked to free them from themselves.

Just like He was for the Israelites, God—the same yesterday, today, and forever—is present in our problems, waiting to fulfill His promises. Now, as then, He is working in the details of our lives, preparing the way for ultimate redemption.

This six-session study, the first in the Storyteller series, is designed to help you:

- Become familiar with a fundamental story in the Old Testament.
- Gain a holistic understanding of the Bible.
- See how the themes of Exodus present themselves throughout the Bible.
- Understand that God is at work even when circumstances seem bleak.